Spotlight on the
SAI story

- When clouds of destruction loom low, the dharma abates.
- When Partha becomes apprehensive, inactive doomed, and despondent, the clarion call of new hope beckons the lost purpose of life.
- Guru incarnates to steer the helm of missionary duty to save, salvage and uplift humanity towards divine goal.

Shri Sai Geetayan

Other works by the same author

Books:

Satya Sai Gaurav (1965)
Satya Sai Gatha (1965)
Bhagawant Dakshinet Avatarale (1965)
Shri Sai Geetayan (1969)
Samarth Gaurav (1980)
Swami Samarth Gaurav Stotra (1983)
Swami Samarth Gaurav Geet (1985)
Realm of Sadhana (1998)
Divine Glory of Shirdi Sai Baba (1998)
Tales from Sai Baba's Life (1998)
Footprints of Sai Baba (1998)
Sai Geetetayan (1998)
Sai Baba Ki Divya Jeevan Kahani (1998)
Sadhana (2000)
Shri Saibabanchi Jeevan Katha (2001)

Poetry:

Kaumudi (1968)
Ganesh Gaurav (1975)
Devi Gaurav (1975)
Swami Samarth Gaurav (1975)
Datta Gaurav (1975)
Chidambar Gaurav (1975)
Buddha Gaurav (1975)
Manik Prabhu Gaurav (1975)
Gatase Geeta Govind (1980)

Songs:

Maharashtra Jaya, Maharashtra Jaya, Jaya Jaya Rashtra Mahan (1960)
Aj Petali Uttar Seema (1964)

Spotlight on the SAI story

Sai Baba and Sadhana

Chakor Ajgaonkar, MA
Ex-Editor 'Saileela'

Sterling Paperbacks

STERLING PAPERBACKS
An imprint of
Sterling Publishers (P) Ltd.
A-59, Okhla Industrial Area, Phase-II,
New Delhi-110020.
Tel: 26387070, 26386209; Fax: 91-11-26383788
E-mail: mail@sterlingpublishers.com
ghai@nde.vsnl.net.in
www.sterlingpublishers.com

Spotlight on the Sai Story
© 2010, Chakor Ajgaonkar, MA
ISBN 978 81 207 4399 1

All rights are reserved.
No part of this publication may be reproduced, stored in a retrieval system or transmitted, in any form or by any means, mechanical, photocopying, recording or otherwise, without prior written permission of the original publisher.

Printed in India
Printed and Published by Sterling Publishers Pvt. Ltd.,
New Delhi-110020.

Preface

The entire life story of Sai Baba is a flow of *amrita* (ambrosia). A drop of the ambrosia illumines and enlightens our entire existence. The shrouded years of Baba's childhood, the suggestive events, dramatic incidents, the enlivening experiences of the devotees, edifying words which Baba spoke, easy but penetrating teachings which transform the core of human life, not only entice our mind and hold us spellbound but also bestow us with new life and insight. They have the aroma, hue, touch, form and illumination of its own.

A small experience of his grace in the struggle of life, the divine help which his love and compassion extend in the moment of agony and suffering, leaves a lasting impression on our mind and soul. We learn that Baba is not fakir but as a *kalpa vriksh* (wish-fulfilling) tree under the shadow of which we have the great fortune to come across.

If we are honest, selfless and loyal devotees, we prostrate before Baba with faith, patience, surrender and dedication. The seeds of karma, bhakti, dhyana and yoga sprout in our mind. We are united with Baba forever and ever. We are endeavouring here to analyse Baba's life glory and philosophy in an artistic and sportive as well as revealing manner with a realistic approach.

These pages present Sai Baba as cosmic awareness of Guruhood descended down on earth to lead human soul to perfection, to lead existence to liberation, to bring unity, equality and amity to religions, nations and humanity, to transform life to inner peace.

The story depicts men and events in chronology, portrays life from spiritual angle, discovers Baba's personality in avataric dimensions of divine Guruhood, exploring new worlds of celestial love and compassion.

14 Girisameep, Srinagar **Chakor Ajgaonkar**
Thane 400604
Telephone: 022-25820180
Mobile: 9324859474

Contents

	Preface	v
1.	Early Years of Sai Baba's Life	1
2.	Sai Baba's Link with Kabir	5
3.	New Light on Early Years (1835–58)	8
4.	Shirdi Is Dwarkavati of Sri Hari!	12
5.	Sai Baba and His Four Mothers!	16
6.	God Incarnates to Taste Mother's Love	21
7.	Light on Years 1858 to 1870	24
8.	Baba Settles in Masjid (1870–80)	31
9.	Visit of Anandanth and Gangagir	36
10.	Shama's Advent and Miracle of Lights	42
11.	Morning of Baba's Sainthood (1880–90)	47
12.	Baba's Begging Round	52
13.	Baba Rejoins His Universal Mission	57
14.	Arrival of Abdulla and Chandorkar	61
15.	Enlightening Nana and Ganu, Harbingers of New Transformation	65
16.	Teaching Imparted to Das Ganu and Chandorkar with Divine Experiences	70
17.	Tenets of Faith and Surrender	77
18.	Baba's Sainthood Rises to Guruhood	80
19.	Universal Guruhood Envelops Devotees from All Quarters	87
20.	Baba's Association with Villagers in Earlier Days	93
21.	Memories of Baba's Early Days and Development of His Divinity	99
22.	Baba Graces Devotees in His Advanced Days	105
23.	Distinguished Personalities in Shirdi Galaxy	112
24.	Guru Purnima (1990) and Essence of Baba's Guru Mahima	120
25.	Purandare's Devotion, Upasani Maharaja's Discipleship and Association of Some Muslim Bhaktas	128
26.	Baba Decides to Merge in His Cosmic Form!	136
27.	Baba Crosses Mundane Borders	143
28.	Guru Incarnation of Love and Compassion Leads Humanity towards Peace and Liberation	148
	Appendix: Sai Baba and Sadhana	157

1

Early Years of Sai Baba's Life

The First Appearance of Sai

It was Baba's nineteenth year when he was seen first under a neem tree in Shirdi in 1854. A bright light was seen under the tree. It was Baba's young face, full of lustre. Baijabai, the loving mother of Tatya Kote Patil, described Baba's face as an orb of light. Baba appeared beneath the tree to respect the memory of his departed father, Guru Roshan Shah Fakir who made his last penance below the tree to cast off his mortal coil and merged in God. It was his Sufi or Kabir cult Guru in whose house Baba was brought up as his son and disciple. Baba stayed under the neem tree for two months and then disappeared for four long years to traverse along the Ajanta–Ellora mountain ranges in Maharashtra and in the Himalayas in northern India. He went to Jhansi during his journey and was a sepoy in Queen of Jhansi's army during the 1857 mutiny against British rule. On his way back, he came to Mangalvedha, Mohol, Akkalkot in Solapur district of Maharashtra to meet with the Dattatreya incarnation of Swami Samarth and return to Shirdi with Chandbhai's nephew's marriage procession. He made a dramatic advent to Shirdi in front of Khandoba Temple where he was greeted as 'Come, Sai Baba' by the Khandoba priest, Mhalsapathi, who later was connected with Baba's life story for years together.

In 1854 when Baba sat as a young fakir below the neem tree, he was admired by the Shirdi village folk as a young sadhu of great penance and austerities. His face glowed with divine illumination. The village folk could not know how and why Baba came to the village and why he sat in meditation under the neem tree for hours together. Baijabai was pained at her heart to see the rigours of the young lad's penance and melted in her bosom to offer him food. Villagers even enquired of the Khandoba *sanchar* (spirit) as to who was the young boy. The man possessed with the sanchar explained that there was the boy's Guru's *turbat* (tomb) below the tree, with whom he had lived for twelve years (1836–48).* Baba practised penance under the same neem tree for twelve years after his arrival from north in 1858. Later he settled in the mosque.

The Saint Buried at Gurusthan

Baba learnt the aulia style of sadhana during his stay with his Guru. He was exemplary of Guru love or Guru bhakti and hence he was aligned to this sacred place throughout his stay at Shirdi for sixty years (1858–1918). He had grown a garden of rose and *zendu* (marigold) near this holy place. He slept in a dust pit behind the Gurusthan. The Buti Mandir pedestal for establishing the image of Krishna was fixed exactly on this pit. Baba selected this pit for his final repose. He desired that his *samadhi* (final repose) be laid on the platform chosen for this idol of Krishna.

Baba was extremely beautiful and lovable with his fair skin and delicate as well as attractive face. My Guru, Dr Ghatwai, had seen Baba in 1911 when he was seventy-six. Ghatwai describes Baba's attractive form and beautiful lustrous face with his white beard bordering his chin, and his palms and feet all pink and soft like that of a young child. We cannot imagine how handsome Baba was in his teenage days when he arrived in Shirdi. The mention of Baba's Guru appears in the work of Swami Sharanananda and Meher Baba mission. It has been stated in the literature that Baba's Guru was connected with the Zar-Zari-Zar Bux (Sufi saint) Dargah at Khuldabad near Aurangabad. This is the exact place of Nath saint Jalandhar Nath. Baba's parents, who lived at Pathari in Parbhani District and were childless until then, had prayed to

---

* Later, Baba confirmed this to Sharanananda. Upasani Baba and Meher Baba were also aware of this.

Jalandhar Nath's samadhi (also the Sufi Dargah) that if they get a child, the child would be offered to the Dargah for service.

The vow yielded children to the couple. After the birth of their first child, Baba, the *mujawar* (fakir) came to Pathari and took the child to his house for teaching him Sufi and Muslim spiritual cult. The fakir was ordained by Allah to make penance under the neem tree in Shirdi, where he died and his grave was laid. After his death, his wife took Baba to the ashram of another Guru, a Hindu Vaishnava saint named Venkusha, at Selu. This saint's real name was Gopal Swami Deshmukh who was an administrator in Nizam state.

Baba's Second Guru (Venkusha)

Baba used to tell his close devotees that if his Guru Venkusha was alive, he could have made all caressing appeals and demands to him. To Dhule Court Commission, Baba has specially mentioned Venkusha's name as his Guru and his cult as Kabir cult. Baba learnt the Vedanta, Geeta, Bhagwat and the Hindu yoga bhakti lore at the feet of Venkusha. Venkusha was a saint of great panache and character who once had a vision that Saint Kabir would be reborn as Sai Baba and would came to his ashram in Selu. Venkusha was also an able administrator in Jintur *pargana* (administrative unit) of Nizam state of nineteenth century.

The Meeting with Swami Samarth

Baba remained in Venkusha's ashram for six years from 1848 to 1854 and first appeared under the neem tree in 1854 to have darshan of his first Guru's samadhi. Thereafter he moved from Shirdi to Ajanta–Ellora mountain ranges and meditated in solitude. He went to northern India and returned to Aurangabad through Mohol, Akkalkot in Solapur district. There he met the Great Dattatreya incarnation as Swami Samarth who directed him to come out of his samadhi state and work for upliftment of people in *sahaj* (natural) samadhi state of being. After this experience of supreme grace, Baba appeared a second time in Shirdi and came to the Khandoba Temple where he was greeted by the priest

Mhalsapathi, who named Baba as 'Sai Baba' (a well-known event in the life story of Baba).

Advent of Baba in Shirdi in 1858

After taking leave from Swami Samarth, Baba came to Aurangabad. In a jungle near the city, a village patil named Chandbhai saw him sitting under a mango tree. Chandbhai had lost his mare in the forest and enquired Baba about it. The latter offered him a *chillum* (smoke pipe) that lit up miraculously and helped him get back his mare. This story is well known to Sai devotees and hence has not been elaborated here. Chandbhai invited Baba to his place, who arrived in Shirdi and was so attracted by the silver surroundings of the Khandoba Temple that he wished to stay on there. However, Mhalsapathi did not allow Baba to climb the steps of the Khandoba Temple because he feared as a Muslim Baba's touch may contaminate the godhead. Baba was pained to note his ignorance and delivered his first historical sermon to Mhalsapathi in front of the temple:

'O, ignorant priest, I am not an idol breaker *yavana* (Muslim). My touch will not render Khandoba unholy, Khandoba is Shiva. He purifies the entire universe. How can my touch contaminate Him? This is your ignorance. Does God dwell in temples and mosques? The entire world is His temple. He cannot be bound by four walls of a building. God has no form, no name; He pervades the entire universe. He does not reside in stones. He resides in the hearts of true devotees, in the *ananda* (bliss) of yogis and in the discrimination of dhyanis. He does not require fruits or flowers. He requires pure hearts surrendered to him and dedicated to human service. God has no religion, cast or creed. I have come to Shirdi to spread this new dawn of knowledge and flow of universal love. Shirdi will be a new window of Love and Truth.' (*Shri Sai Geetayan*)*

This was Baba's first immortal sermon delivered in Shirdi, which reflected his life mission.

---

* An original Marathi lyrical series depicting Sai's life and teachings in songs and music, written by Shri Chakor Ajgaonkar, published by Diamond Book.

2

Sai Baba's Link with Kabir

Message of Unity of All Godheads, All Sects and Creeds

Mid-nineteenth century was rife with the concepts of caste, creed, sect and religion, and infested with evils of discrimination throughout the society. Even today when the world has progressed in industry, education and scientific fields, the inequality and intolerance has not ended; not even diminished. It is, in fact, taking new political and social dimensions. The revolutionary thoughts and deeds of Baba were far ahead of his contemporary society. That Allah is malik, all humanity is one and equal at all levels of life, was the essence of Baba's experience and spiritual philosophy. The central point around which his philosophy revolved was that God does not live in temples or mosques; he lives in the heart of his devotees. He can be appeased by love alone. He loves the offering of a pure, loving, dedicated heart and surrendered ego. These same thoughts were championed by a revolutionary and visionary saint named Kabir some four hundred years ago. This was the reappearance of Kabir whose lifespan was 1435–1518 as against Sai's lifetime 1835–1918. Both were rebel visionary saints of secular humanitarian principles based on equality of human beings in India.

Vision of Venkusha, Baba's Second Guru

Venkusha was said to be the reincarnation of Ramanand Maharaj of Varanasi (Kashi). This saint was on pilgrimage to holy places with a group of his disciples. He once came to the Ahmedabad Dargah of Pir Subagshah, and the walls of the Dargah perspired! It was a miracle. Subagshah was thus greeting Gopal Swami (Venkusha). He recognized the divine sign and communicated with the soul of the Pir, who revealed to the Swami that he was Ramanand, the Vaishnava saint of Kashi and his choicest disciple Kabir was to take birth soon near Manwat in Parbhani.

The Pir told Gopal Swami that he should wind up his pilgrimage and go back to his ashram to receive and train the new incarnation of his disciple. And truly so, Baba was taken by his first Guru's wife to Venkusha's ashram were he was trained for six years. Baba is said to have been led to the presence of Lord Dattatreya in fakir form at Malanga Gad by Roshan Shah, his first fakir Guru. The other higher education in karma, dhyana (meditation), bhakti (devotion) and yoga was enjoined to young Sai by Venkusha. Thus Baba became perfect in the comprehensive spiritual philosophy of Hindu–Muslim and all Indian spiritual styles and processes. His philosophy of comprehensive secularism is reflected in his sermon to Mhalsapathi in front of Khandoba Temple. Its message, however, has not been properly appreciated because nobody has studied and analysed the life and message of Sai in correct depth, extension or latitude for a picturization or depiction as a biographical form.

Kabir and Sai Incarnations

The unity of both saints is not only an atmic conception but also based on social equality and equity. The lifestyle is extremely parallel and resembling. The liberal message of human equality cannot be easily forgotten. This indicates possibility of rebirth of the same *atma* (self) of Kabir as Sai. Baba used to tell his close followers that he was weaving garments on the bank of Ganges. The Rama's name which was given to Kabir as a mantra was resounding in the blood and veins of Sai. Mhalsapathi, Kote Patil and Shama had heard the name of Rama echoing in Baba's heart. Baba had allowed to start celebration of Ram Navami in Shirdi from 1911. Baba used to respect the two Hanuman idols at Shanipur. He sat below the level of the feet of Hanuman, saying, 'How can I sit at the same level of God?' When anybody asked him about his parentage, he used to point out his finger at the two idols and say, 'He is my parent, do not enquire any more.' In Chawdi procession later, Baba was possessed with mighty and uncontrollable sanchar in front of Maruti Temple.

Baba's Love for His Guru

The symbolism of loyalty towards one's Guru was an exemplary trait of Sai Baba. The grace of Guru is the main lever which turns the entire life into the ecstasy of realization. This *shakti* (power) of Guru was symbolized in Sai Baba. He himself personified the power of his Guru in fakir form; moving from age to age, century to century, helping his devotees. Baba's experiences, as narrated by him in his tales to the devotees, indicate that he was operative for a thousand years before he incarnated as Sai Baba.

New Light on Early Years (1835–58)

Fakir Roving through Ages

Sai Baba's personality and tenets have the stamp of *sadhana* (penance) of Kabir, Sufi, Nath, Datta and the Bhagwat cult. The great message given by Baba on the Kabir style that God is one and real religion is humanitarian love and compassion is well known. Baba, like Kabir, held the opinion that God does not reside in temples or mosques. His real resting-place is the pure heart of a *bhakta* (devotee), equipoise of a *dhyani* (meditator), dedication of a *karmanistha* (karma believer) and the divine ananda of a merged yogi. Bhaktas have carved a universal image of Baba in their hearts that he is moving from age to age, from century to century, disseminating his message of unity, equality, love and compassion coupled with his celestial and munificent grace.

One more facet of Baba's personality was the influence of the tenets of both Hindu and Muslim religions and spiritual sadhanas. They were so perfectly mixed that both Hindus and Muslims held him as their own holy man. Baba's earlier years were shrouded with mystery because he never expressed his identity in terms of caste, creed, sect, religion, family, race, birthplace or parentage. His aim was to lift his own followers above the rampant differences and discriminations and fix them in the appropriate altitude of unity, equality and brotherhood. The touch of divine and the embodiment of Guru's own shakti which was personified in Sai Baba could never be bound by external boundaries and he had no reason to follow the wrong and unjust way of thinking, prevalent in contemporary society. He was born to bathe the lives of his devotees in the ambrosial showers of love, compassion and the enlightening grace, which flowed from his prowess as a perfect and accomplished Master (Siddha). This is the line separating him from the Bhagwat saints in Maharashtra. The level of unity and equality professed by Maharashtra's saints remained mainly on the atmic or spiritual level. Baba's approach of equality was deeper and more imprinted on day-to-day life and experience. He walked on the dusty paths of society and was very practical. His siddha shakti was instantly effective like that of Lord Datta in Shripad Shrivallabh form Guruhood with depth of compassion which was expressive in Shatrpad incarnation of Lord Dattatreya.

Search-Lights Focussed on Earlier Life

Of Baba's earlier life, devotees tell that he used to enquire about some prominent personalities or saints and aulias in Pathari, Selu, Manawat and Aurangabad as well. This indicated his close contact as also interest in the areas and personalities with which he had contact in the earlier years. He referred to Roshan Shah Fakir and Satguru Venkusha who were his Gurus in his younger days. He used to tell that he asked for *dakshina* (token fee) only from those whom the fakir, the indweller of the mosque, had directed him to demand. He also referred to Dattaguru who asked for things from devotees who visited the mosque. Kabir and Sufi sadhana was given to him by his first Guru who seemed to be linked with the Sufi Dargah as well as the Kabir cult. The sadhana of siddha nama (mantra given by Guru) and Nadanusandhana (hearing primeval Om) were enjoined to him through Kabir-style saints. The love for Guru and loving God (as the beloved) form the Sufi culture. He was also taught the siddha path of raising mind to *unmana* (no-mind) stage by merging body consciousness, mind, intellect and ego in God. The style of Venkusha was dhyana, bhakti, yoga and karma with Vaishnava devotion of dedication and surrender. All the traits of Hindu–Muslim styles of sadhana were confluenced in Sai Baba, which made him a Perfect Master or Poorna Satguru. Meher Baba's description of Baba in his literature as Perfect Master is apt and absolutely true.

Developments in Pathari in Recent Years

Great personalities connected with Baba, viz. Swami Sharanananda, Das Ganu, Meher Baba, Digambar Swami (Vajreshwari) have evidence to believe that Sai Baba was born in Pathari (Parbhani district). His birth date was 28 September 1835, as per Sathya Sai Baba. The Panchayat Samiti had built one hall in Baba's memory in Pathari. An inscription of Baba's parents' names was found in Pathari as per Dr Bhusari, a descendant of Sai Baba's family. Devotees have built a mandir in Pathari worth Rs 25 lakhs with the help of a millionaire from Tamil Nadu. We have nothing to do with these evidences here, except a passing mention. We have to collect amrita drops from Baba's life and philosophy, which remained to be properly highlighted in past. During his travel to North India, he had gone up to Himalayan ranges. He used to say that he had seen the 1857 war of independence. He was then in the army of Rani Laxmibai of Jhansi. He left the army after the fall of the Queen of Jhansi. He had also been one of the followers of the great Datta incarnation Swami Samarth of Akkalkot. He used to refer to the great incarnation as 'Sarkar' and referred to his feet as 'God's feet'.

While Baba was in the Jhansi army, Swami Samarth used to arrange wooden sticks and say that he was organizing army battalions. The Swami took care of Baba during the days of Indian mutiny. Later, the devotees of Swami were ordained by a vision that he was at Shirdi and his *padukas* (footwear) need be taken to Shirdi instead of Akkalkot. A devotee named Dr Ramrao Kothari established Swami's padukas below the Gurusthan under the direction of Upasani Maharaj. Baba's style of grace was based on Datta incarnation Shripad Shrivallabha's style of compassion and succour to his devotees. This thread of Datta style is woven in Sai Baba's entire lifestyle.

Baba's encounter with Chandbhai in 1858, in a jungle near Aurangabad, was a prelude to his appearance in Shirdi village for a second time to settle there for a lifelong sojourn. The events that unfolded laid a deep impression in his mind that Baba was a great aulia. He begged at Baba's feet to accept his invitation to visit his home to Dhupkheda. Baba obliged him later.

Baba Arrived in Shirdi with the Marriage Processions

One day, when a marriage procession from Chandbhai's house was to proceed to Shirdi, Baba graced Chandbhai with his auspicious visit. Chand's wife's nephew had his bride at Shirdi and the marriage party was to go to attend the wedding ceremony. The party arrived on the outskirts of Shirdi in the early morning hours. Baba was attracted by the sylvan surrounding of the jungle area around the Khandoba Temple of the olden days. He left the party and proceeded to the mandir. The further incident of Mhalsapathi greeting the young fakir as 'Sai Baba' is well known to all. The great historical message of unity of godheads, religion of humanity and dwelling of God in human heart emanated from Baba's mouth in 1858 in front of Khandoba Temple. This was the heritage of Kabir, brought forward by Baba in this new *avatar* (incarnation)! Baba was really an extension of Kabir and his philosophy running into mid-nineteenth century India.

'The God does not dwell in masjid or mandir. He is not bound by four walls of a shrine. He is the dweller of Universe as well as the heart of a true devotee.'

(Shri Sai Geetayan)

4

Shirdi Is Dwarkavati of Shri Hari!

Settling Down at Shirdi

We have discussed Baba's advent in Shirdi, once in 1854 and again in 1858. Let us now think of Shirdi and the significance of Baba's coming to this place of historical and cultural backdrop.

Baba, in the four years of his pilgrimage, travelled to mountain ranges surrounding Ajanta–Ellora caves, Zar-Zari-Zar Bux Dargah, Eknath Maharaj's Guru's place (Daulatabad fort), Khuldabad, Aurangabad, Dattatreya and Nath saints' shrines and samadhis, Pandharpur, Akkalkot, Chakra Teertha in Himalayas, Uttar Pradesh, Madhya Pradesh, Himachal Pradesh, Jhansi, Vindhya ranges, Satpura Hills, Nasik and nearby Ram *teerthas* (pilgrim places), and other sacred places near the banks of Narmada and Godavari rivers. He at last negotiated and settled in Shirdi, which was not far from the bank of Godavari, where his Guru (Roshan Shah) had his final repose.

Cultural Heritage of Shirdi

Shri Sai Geetayan describes Baba's coming to Shirdi in poetically inspired words as follows:

'Shri Hari has assumed the form of Sai Ram on the banks of Godavari River. This river relished the sacred company of Nath and Bhagwat saints. Shri Ram had stayed with his consort, Sita, on the banks of Godavari and passed his holy days and nights in her company. This Godavari pours pitchers of devotion to the doors of philosophy of unity of God and his loving devotees. Godavari is a stream of illumined philosophy lighting dark recesses of ignorance!'

We have examined Baba's aspect of glory as Guru for higher aspirants. We have also seen his sportive Krishna form which fascinates his householder and *sansari* (wordly) devotees. Baba also confirms his Krishna form by calling Shirdi as Dwarka or Dwarkavati, the auspicious abode of Lord Krishna. He lived in a mosque which he named the Dwarkamai. He wished that his body should be reposed on the platform where Lord Krishna's idol was to be installed in Buti Mandir. It has been said in *Sai Geetayan*:

'Sai, the Shri Hari incarnation, has manifested on the Godavari bank. It also described Shirdi as Vaikunthapuri and Sai Baba as Shyamasunder Hari. Baba with his auspicious *leelas* (acts) and stay has rendered Shirdi a place of pilgrimage, like Kashi, Rameshwar, Pandharpur. Sai used to play his divine leelas among the poor village folk of Shirdi as Lord Krishna sported with cowherds. He is quoted as saying that the mosque is the bhaktas auspicious Dwarka, the dwelling place of Lord Krishna. The Lord who is great yogi of Kailasa (Shiva), has to come down as Krishna for the benefit of his simple, ignorant devotees. He has to embrace them to heart and uplift them above the material strata or level.'

This Shirdi Is Dwarka

Baba has unerringly told that Shirdi is the place where the puranic Dwarka of Shri Krishna existed. The present Dwarka in Saurashtra is a later creation by the Lord on the behest of saints, sages, rishis and munis. Sai Baba says that Shirdi is Dwarka; Dwarkavati is inherent of a deeper mythical, cultural and historical truth. Baba, through his mystic insight into the past, knows that the real ancient puranic Dwarka existed in the area surrounding the place where present Shirdi is situated. It is said that the original Dwarka (at the south of the Vindhya ranges) was submerged in the sea by Lord Krishna on the eve of onset of Kali Yuga. Instead there emerged the Dwarasamudra or Ksheersagar (a sea of saltless waters). Dr Gavankar[*], in his famous book *Shiladhi*, has given historical

---

[*] An erstwhile Trust head of Shirdi Sansthan.

and puranic evidences of this fact. The Ksheersagar existed in Maharashtra, Karnataka and Telangana area of Southern India. Such districts of Maharashtra as Ahmednagar, Satara, Solapur, etc have the evidence of this sea being churned by the gods and demons to get amrita as well as the *ratnas* (gems).

The name Dwarkavati or Dwarasamudra seems to be derived from Dwarkanagari of Lord Shri Krishna. It is therefore proved that the divine incarnation of 'Sai' Krishna had selected this modern Dwarka as his habitat.

The Ratnas Related to This Area

The villages and towns around the Dwarasamudra are named after various ratnas emerging from the sea. The name of Vishnu's Mohini form is also related with the 'Samudra Manthana' (the churning of the sea). Mohiniraj Temple is near Newasa. The severed head of Rahu whom Vishnu had slain lies in the temples of Rahu and Ketu. The Rahuri town is named after Rahu. Ratangad is having the memory of Ketu. Lord Shiva who drank the venom 'Halahal' is seen as Mhatar Dev at Vriddheshwar (Old Shankar). Indra's Bilweshwar (Belapur), Ashwini Kumara's Ashwi, Chandra's Chandreshwar Mahadeo, Surya's Kolhar (Viwasvan) Temples are situated in the adjacent areas. This has been discussed by Dr Gavankar in his two famous books on Sai Baba's life. It is not intended to pile up evidence of puranic lore to establish a historical truth. We intend to point out here Baba's awareness of the legendary, historical and cultural links of Shirdi to old times. Baba was Shyamasunder Krishna for his bhaktas. It is therefore understood that he is Shri Krishna reincarnated and his abode Dwarka. This aspect was adored by his innumerable followers whose prime intention was to fulfil their desires and longings first through the grace of an evolved Master i.e. Guru. God likes not only high-souled renounced dhyana yogis but also his materialistic devotees. He has to assume a face to cater to such bhaktas of his own. God forsakes none of his bhaktas, irrespective of their high or low status.

The Leela Stay in Mosque

Baba desired to realign his Krishna aspect through this Dwarkavati Dwarka Masjid in Shirdi. This leela-form carried the fragrance of his divinity and compassion beyond Ahmednagar district to Maharashtra and beyond India into the wide expanse of global appreciation and following. Shirdi became not only an Indian pilgrim centre, but also a universal source of love, knowledge and divine compassion. The life of Sai Baba has the sacredness of Ganga and Yamuna, depth of the Indian Ocean and the loftiness of the Himalayas. However, because he selected Shirdi as his karma *bhoomi* (land), his life was first bound within the geographical frame of Maharashtra. Baba was nourished in the terrain of Sahyadri and its ridged landscape. He has moved in the soil conserved by Godavari and Bhima where Bhagwat saints have lived their lives and spread their philosophy of dhyana bhakti. Baba has lived in the land where the Nath saints and Masters have flourished and nurtured their glory from dust to sky canopy. Baba is, therefore, originally a Marathi Siddha. He later became universal, yet he spoke a language which was of local Marathi dialect spoken by the rural rustic folk in Maharashtra. Bhagwat saints were fed on grace from Nath Siddhas. They parted the lustre and glory in favour of rustic common Warkari Folk of Pandharpur Bhakti Cult. Baba imparted his siddha power and almighty process to the Bhakti Philosophy of Maharashtra. Baba looked like a yogi, Sthitapradnya Gunateeta, dhyani bhakta of Geeta. But he was at once a Siddha or Perfect Master and descended from divine; illumining the entire universal sky with love and compassion.

Sai Baba and His Four Mothers!

We have collected some drops of amrita from Sai's life by spotlighting some unknown footprints from his earlier life. We have tried to understand the Guruhood of incarnating Master and the process of origin and growth, and also the leelas he played for the welfare and upliftment of the ignorant and drifting household devotees enrapt in meshes of the *sansar* (world).

The Formless Assumes Form

The original substance of universal Brahma cannot be fettered in any kind of name or form. However the purport of such a principle cannot be understood by common people without the medium of name and form. It is therefore that the universal power is born as Swami Samarth or Sai Baba, the epoch-making human incarnations. The devotees have their unquenched thirst to see the divine in person from birth to birth, even sadhus and saints pant for the divine to unfold itself on the bank of river of time. The God has to then incarnate to fulfil their sublime wishes. As clouds of destruction loom low on the battlefield, Arjuna becomes apprehensive and despondent. The clarion call of hope for new life revives the humanity to steer the helm of duty through an epoch-making divine incarnation such as Sai Baba. God incarnates in every age to establish dharma, hence destroying wicked tendencies and protecting men of righteous purpose. Baba thus appeared in Maharashtra in 1835. The *Sai Geetayan* describes this poetically:

'The primeval word "Om" has surged from limitless expanse of the cosmos. The formless assumes form on earth. The universal God out of love of devotees has come down to a village in Maharashtra to answer the yearnings of those who loved and cherished him. He is just the personified grace of eternal Guru Lord Dattatreya. The feet of Baba are the same which have made their imprints on the bank of Sharayu and Yamuna; those have traversed through forests as well as marble floors of palaces, whether in exile or in the majestic darbar halls. These feet have chosen to tread on the paths of Shirdi hamlet full of rough and hot dust. The godliness of divine has flowered in the mundane earthen soil. The earth has raised its dust to touch the aroma of celestial height. The unknown has met the known. He who is the unknown source behind the manifested creation, the unseen basis of the seen universe, the magic parade of the supportless Brahma, has appeared on the planet earth. The opportunity of meeting the Lord is rare. It will not reappear. O devoted and righteous people in the world, be wakeful and alert. Hold fast to the Lord's feet, Lord who is receiver of the unmixed ananda, source of ecstasy and bliss, the Guru or the marvellous Sarkar.'

'Brahma Is My Father and Maya My Mother'

The advent of Sai Baba in Shirdi set up a stage for the spreading of true spiritual light on the genuine bhaktas who had strayed away from the glorious goal due to misconceptions, misguidance and lack of authentic Guru, guide and comrade. The miraculous identity of Baba as a ray of the universal light could be manifested in his words, actions and mysterious happenings at his will. Somebody was bold enough to ask him about his parentage and he replied back instantly that Brahma was his father and Maya his mother. This is verifying the truth about incarnations because they take birth through their free will by contracting the forces of Prakriti (Nature). They have no selfish purpose to gratify. They come for the welfare and succour of humanity. Swami Samarth and Baba used to reply in the same strain. Brahma was his father and Amba was his mother. Krishna has also declared that he has no karma to perform on earth. Yet he moulds the matrix of *maya* (illusion) and comes on earth to establish the way of righteousness, spirituality and godward progress of mankind. Taking this sublime process in view, Baba never disclosed to people around him that he belonged to Bhusari family in Pathari (Parbhani), his father was Hariharpant and his mother Girijabai. A stream named Lendi flowed from the backyard of his ancestral house, and Lord Hanuman was the family deity of his Bhusari family. Basically, incarnations have no birthplace, parentage, kith and kin, caste, religion, creed. Baba had to show a new way to the world, which consisted of no divisions of caste and religion, where humanity was the singular religious faith and compassion of Siddha—a way of life—as the rightful approach to the worldly struggle. Baba disclosed his identity before the daily visiting common folk, men of position and authority, educated as well as rustic villagers around. He wanted his timeless eternity to be understood and recognized. His name was Sai Baba, but it filled the context of his timeless avatarhood virtually; he had the compassion of father, love of mother and the power and glory of God blended in his personality. He was therefore loved by his followers as mightier than God, compassionate than the father and more loving than the mother. As he used the power of Brahma (i.e. Prakriti's forces) to help his bhaktas, he called Dwarkamai the Mother. He represented the world of destiny which shapes the ends of men and women according to their karmas but protects those among them who rely on their Guru or God, who are ever surrendered to the Lord. The destiny had no power over Guru bhaktas. The Prakriti is ordered by the Guru principle to protect the devoted and dedicated sons of God.

Fakir Father, Mosque Mother

Roshan Shah Fakir in the mosque was his father and Guru, hence Baba obeyed whatever the fakir directed him to do and he in turn demanded it from the devotees. He used to deliver or offer the object asked by the fakir through Dwarkamai. Whenever the dakshina reached the fakir, the destiny was controlled by the prakriti power. The devotee found his difficulties solved, his mind attained peace, the *jiva* (individual self) was uplifted. Baba never asked anything for himself. His every word, act and deed was for the welfare of his dear devotees. It was stuffed with Dhyanah Vedantic truth. The stream of amrita from Geeta and Bhagwat flowed from his actions. The divine son of the celestial parents was full of paradoxes. Baba used to stay in the masjid but he made a mandir out of it by hanging a bell in it. His *dhuni* (sacred fire) was worship of fire. The confluence of all Hindu–Muslim styles of living, acting and teaching was embedded in his own life. He used to wear rags, but Laxmi was at his service. He sat on a mat, lived on begging but was plentiful as a monarch. He asked for dakshina but nothing would be left after he had distributed the money to the destitutes. He expressed his rage in pitched voice and harsh words but he was himself an example of utter self-control. The entire Vedantic truth was at his commands. His heart melted with love and compassion. He was not a householder but he carried the burdens of the householder devotees on his own shoulders. He sat at one place but touched the entire universe. He had no parents but was the father and mother of the entire humanity. To love human beings was his religion. He taught not only in words but also through suggestive actions, events and miracles in an indirect and mystic way. He left his mortal coil to save a faith brother. Baba had come to Shirdi to teach a human being his true religion and true self. He was launching a new movement of dawning knowledge, edification and upliftment of human soul on the horizon of devotee world. This flame from the cosmos had alighted on earth to tread the dust of Shirdi. So that the soul can rise up to the state of universal consciousness, stepping on the ladder of divine grace which had by chance come to the village of Shirdi, which was never before known to the world.

Baba and His Four Mothers

If we say that Sai Baba had four mothers, all his devotees will be utterly surprised. It is because nobody knows of any of his mothers at all. These four mothers had a significant place in Baba's known and unknown life. His first mother was none else than the Dwarkamai. He called the Dwarkamai Masjid as his own mother as well as the compassionate mother of all living beings, whom she always protected from dangers of destiny and maya. Those who climbed her steps were relieved from the fetters of karmas and pranks of *prarabdha* (destiny). This was the mother on whose lap sat 'Sai' Krishna. She used to sing lullabies and make him sleep in peace. She was wielding all eight powers or siddhis. Her divine magic enabled Baba to light lamps using water instead of oil. She was the mother who enabled Baba to control five elements. When the village of Shirdi was hit by a hurricane, with tempestuous wind blowing and heavy downpour of stormy rains battering the village houses, she was the seat of Baba from where he saved his bhaktas, crossing the limits of distance and time. Once, he saved a blacksmith's child from being burnt in the fire by inserting his own hand in the dhuni. From this very seat he saved Kashiram Shimpi when he was attacked by robbers on his way back from market. It was here that Baba convinced Das Ganu that he was both Shiva and Vishnu with the Ganges flowing in fountains of water from his divine feet. For the sansari people, he was Vishnu and for the dhyanis he was Shiva himself. The three gods are one and Baba had reconciled the duality of Hari and Hara. He saved Tatya Kote's life by offering his own life as substitute. This power of *parabrahma* (supreme), this maya shakti of prakriti and *purusha* (human form) was symbolically represented by Dwarka Mother of Sai. She was Adi Maya, the mother of all the three worlds. She was the Anagha Shakti of Guru, Lord Dattatreya. She was Lalita or Tripura Shakti, the supreme power, which made Baba 'Satchitananda' Satguru. She gave relief to the one great Master who lived and sported in the masjid for his divine work and mission. The other mothers of Baba were—one who gave birth to him; the fakir's wife who reared him as her own son for twelve years; and the meritorious lady living in Shirdi, who took care of him during his young days—Baijabai Kote Patil.

God Incarnates to Taste Mother's Love

We have extensively elucidated how Baba had four mothers, one of which was symbolical mother Dwarkamai Masjid, the protective mother of all the bhaktas. Baba also called her symbolic Shakti of Guru (the Adi Shakti) which governs, moulds and shapes the destiny of humanity. Let us now refer to the remaining three mothers.

Second Mother

This was Baba's real mother, who carried him in her womb as a grace endowed upon the parents by Jalandhar Nath shrine. Her name is said to be Girijabai. Though some say she was Avantikabai, and some Devgiri Amma. But let us not stumble across names. She was verily the pious, God fearing, pure and auspicious lady whose merits made her carry Baba's celestial body inside her. Baba never disclosed his parentage because he wanted to maintain his secular mission untarnished by parentage, race, caste and religion. Digambar Swami and Meher Baba, who were Siddhas themselves, believed that Baba's name was 'Atmaram', the first child of Hariharpant and Girijabai couple from Bhusari family of Pathari in Parbhani district. The couple was destined not to have any issue. However, a vow to the powerful Sufi Dargah at Khuldabad earned them progeny, which as a precondition to vow, they had to part with. In the olden days, it was a practice for issueless parents to take vows before the samadhis of saints and surrender the begotten child to the pir or sadhu for the propagation of his faith. Girijabai, who bore him in her womb, had the very acid test to undergo. She had to part with her beautiful, newborn son to honour the vow. How pained would her heart have been in the agony of losing the divine child to respect the commitment of faith! What self-control, self-determination and the sacrifice she would have had to undergo! The child was given to the priest of the Dargah, namely Roshan Shah Fakir, who reared Baba in his household for twelve years and enjoined to him not only Sufi sadhana but also *darshan* (vision) of Dattatreya. Thereafter Baba lived in Venkusha's ashram for six years and later travelled across the Indian subcontinent for four years. His stay in Shirdi for sixty long years earned him the fame of an incarnation. But his parents remained unknown to the devotees and outside world.

Baba's Third Mother

Baba's third mother was Roshan Shah's wife who nurtured him from his first year up to his twelfth year in her household while the fakir trained him in various tenets. Baba always remembered the fakir and his wife while he stayed at Shirdi. The tomb of Baba's Guru lay under the neem tree, where he used to sit in meditation. He used to refer to his Guru as his fakir. Many times, he was referred to as the fakir of all fakirs, Lord Dattatreya, the eternal Guru, whom Roshan Shah introduced to Baba on Malang God. After the fakir left his body, this third mother took Baba to Venkusha's ashram where he was greeted by the saint as 'My Shiva has come'. He allowed the lady also to stay in Selu and earn her livelihood.

Baba's Fourth Mother

Mother Baijabai came in Baba's life during his stay at Shirdi from 1858 onwards, when he used to spend hours in intense meditation in the jungle. Baba was oblivious of all his physical needs and moved barefoot, caring very little for his day-to-day needs and also basic requirements to put together body and soul. He had been separated from his original parents in infancy and reared in strict discipline of Roshan Shah's spiritual training. He must have played very little with his toddler and teenage friends. The hardships of the self-denying rigorous discipline and the spiritual practices were noticed by the loving Baijabai. She saw him below the neem tree as an orb of sun rising up the horizon. She melted with love, compassion and affection of a true mother. People have no knowledge of the closeness of his two mothers Girijabai and the fakir lady. But they are aware of the closeness of Baija mother, as she roamed searching Baba on the thorny and rigid paths in the jungle and fed him with morsels of bread and onion. Zunka/bread and puran poli she brought with her is still fragrant in Shirdi to this date. Baba used to ward off Baija mother saying that he had left his house and parents to keep away from Maya and worldly affections. He never wanted her to entangle him in worldly love and bonds of motherly affection. But Baija mother's love and dedication was so great that he could not resist her approaches, which were mixed with devotion and regard. Mother's love is so powerful that it invades a fakir son as well as God. God himself desires to taste motherly love. He has no mother; he himself is the mother of universe. He has to incarnate as the Ram of Kausalya or Krishna of Yashoda to taste the love of a mother. It is because of this that Baba had to yield to the motherly love of Baijabai and accept her feelings of *vatsalya* (motherly) bhakti. He rewarded Baija with the darshan of Vishnu in her last moments. He saved her son Tatya Kote Patil to compensate his mother's love. Baba accepted the death of Tatya for himself and kept him alive in his sickness. The episode of Baija is great and illustrious in Sai story. When Baija died Baba wept as a child and said, 'My Tatya's mother has gone, my Mami is no more.' He was a Sthitapradnya yogi renouncing the world of mayic affections. However, he became a child before the divine love of Baija mother. Salute to the worthy mother and her son Sai Baba!

Light on Years 1858 to 1870

In the last six episodes, we have viewed Sai Baba's life with the warmth of love, faith, devotion, as well as analytical reasoning against the backdrop of Indian spiritual thought. We have also weighed the place of Baba in the task of uplifting humanity and his concrete contribution to the mysticism of the ancient land. We have searched the obscure paths of his childhood and youthful exuberance that the earlier authors of his biography left untouched. These include his stay in the house of his Sufi and Vaishnava Gurus during 1835 to 1854; his appearance under the neem tree in 1854 and reappearance in front of Khandoba Shrine in 1858. His link with Kabir avatar and the purpose of his new incarnation as Sai Baba. We have discussed historical and cultural background of Shirdi village as also the aura of motherhood in Baba's life. We have now to probe into the next segment of his life and live with him along his sainthood light and glory in these obscure years.

Kashiram Shimpi and Appa Jagle were Mhalsapathi's friends and regular visitors of Khandoba Temple. They were witness to the divine message of unity given by Baba in front of the temple. When he arrived in Shirdi for the second time after completing his journey in northern India, these two souls guided Baba to the neem tree and the old masjid. Baba thus came to settle in Shirdi precincts when he had already completed twenty-three years of his life. The dawn in Baba's life had ended here and the morning light was glimmering in the forest surrounding old Shirdi in mid-nineteenth century. The next twenty years (1858–78) are also shadowed by lack of information in such a measure that these days are neither under darkness of night nor under visibility of sunshine. We are trying to present Baba in a chronological flow of years.

Hemadpant and Narasimha Swami

The first among Baba's biographer was Shri Annasaheb Dabholkar (or Hemadpant) whose work is respected and recited as a religious *pothi* (book) by the Sai devotees worldwide. Hemadpant had come to Shirdi in 1909, when Baba was well-recognized in Maharashtra, and Shirdi was fairly visited by educated and well-to-do persons from neighbouring towns and cities. Baba allowed Hemadpant to keep a record of the experiences of devotees in his life. It was a limited purpose and the events are not evenly or chronologically recorded. But the book is held as authoritative by all Marathi as well as non-Marathi devotees of Sai Baba. Dabholkar was a government officer and he was well versed in saint biographies and also Indian philosophy, which has been reflected in the collection of experiences by him. This is not 'Charitra' in real sense. His analytical mind has been bridled by Baba by calling him 'Arguing' Hemadpant (philosopher). He has commented on sporadic events and incidents in Baba's life without logic or reason, accepting everything with surrendered faith. The episodes in his book are treasure for devotees but they are not resources for a biography examined with insight of genius and chronology of historical and scientific approach. The next recognizable biography is of Narasimha Swamiji of All India Sai Samaj (Chennai), who was an eminent lawyer, patriot and logicist and in Annie Besant's Home Rule agitation. He was in Tilak's Swaraj campaign. He was in a different section of *sadhakas* (mystical and aspirant souls), who were from the lineage of Meher Baba, Ramana Maharshi, Upasani Maharaj and was therefore more practical as well as spiritual man. He unceasingly moved in Maharashtra to collect data on Sai Baba and his life. He analysed the psychology of Baba's eminent and well-known householder devotees. His way of analysis of Sai Baba and his life was deeper and his understanding of Baba's philosophy was all embracing. Hence, his works are more acceptable to the learned and aspirant devotees worldwide. The works of Das Ganu are full of poetical love but are very brief. Narasimha Swamiji has written Baba's life in four volumes. We have to read all new books on Baba's life and present him and his philosophy in the proper perspective. This sequence on Baba's life allows us to view him in poetical depth, philosophical backdrop, yogic and aspirant's approach and create an atmosphere of proper appreciation, understanding of his life so that a devotee not only remains a devotee but becomes an aspirant on sadhana path as well. Baba himself desired this transformation in his followers.

Partially Visible Years in Sai Baba's Life

This period is demarcated by two milestones in Baba's life. The period of twelve years from 1858 to 1870 when Baba was yet to settle in his Dwarkamai abode, and again from 1870 to 1878 when he came to settle in the mosque and manifested his divinity after departure of the great Dattatreya incarnation of Swami Samarth of Akkalkot. These twenty years are obscure because the distinct and well-known miracles in Sai Baba's life were manifested after Swami's samadhi in 1878. He was not known beyond Shirdi and Ahmednagar until he lighted lamps in the old mosque using water instead of oil. Very little is known to Baba's biographers about this period because recordable miracles did not accrue during these twenty years, when Baba slept in the dust pit behind the neem tree at night and wandered in forest barefooted and spent hours in meditation and rigorous penance. We are turning our attention to this period to make our readers and fellow devotees visualize to some extent the segment of Sai Baba's life as reflected in this dusky period of obscurity. This period is indeed the making of Baba's sainthood and is most important in understanding his personality and mission. Baba was, until 1870, not staying or sleeping in the masjid. He spent his time in the forest, amidst shrubs and the cactus growth, in solitude, meditating under the neem tree on the turbat of his Sufi Guru. He became resplendent through his repose at night in the pit behind his Guru's samadhi and the penance under the neem tree casting its shadow on the tomb of his Guru. The neighbouring villagers came to know of his illumination even through the thick mist of his non-recognition.

The 1858 Shirdi, Shrouded by Tall Trees, Dense Forests, Cactus Islands

The Shirdi of those days was green and enlivened by rich forest growth all around. The village seemed to be a waten in old days because it was surrounded by an earthen wall all around. The northern part of the wall was broken and the neem tree known as Baba's Gurusthan was sprouting from the fallen remains of the village fortification. The village was formed out of grass huts, roofed houses built in open areas within the tree growth. The Khandoba Temple was a picture of greenery and silent repose. The village pathways were seen leading to the village from the temple precincts. The Guru's place was encircled by thickets, forest shrubs, tall trees and thorny growth. The piece of land between the mosque and the neem tree was full of dense trees and thorny creepers. The scorpions, serpents and other poisonous insects were freely moving in the area. The Samadhi Mandir was erected at this place after sixty years (i.e. a few days prior to Baba's own samadhi). Buti had to acquire the land, cut the forest and clean the area in order to lay foundation of the proposed Krishna Mandir.

Baba loved the neem tree very intensely because his Guru who nurtured and moulded his personality was lying in the tomb beneath it. Baba had seen the old dilapidated masjid (which was later known as Dwarkamai) but his mind did not find peace there at first. He was more tranquil, peaceful and bliss-oriented in the proximity of his Guru. The sky was his blanket and the earth was his bed during these early days of his sojourn at Shirdi. He used to remember the love and grace of his guardian and Guru Roshan Shah Fakir, whose house was his resort in his early childhood. By the year 1870, however, Baba reconciled himself to the routine life of the masjid.

The Shade of Guru Grace below Neem

It appears that Baba's Guru gave him the order or command to stop roaming in the hot sun, rain showers and winter cold after his penance of twelve long years. Even when he came to live in the mosque, he still adored his Guru's samadhi. He used to pour water on rose and marigold plants, which he grew near the place in honour of his Guru. He had now been ordained to mix among society and help the poor and needy so that their faith in Allah is confirmed. Occasionally visiting the Dwarkamai mosque, Baba spent his time during the day under neem and wandering in the dense forest for the rest of the day, oblivious of his tiredness or hunger as also other corporal exigencies. At night he would retire to the dusty pit behind his Guru's samadhi. The men and women in Shirdi developed an attitude of admiration and respect for the young saint who loved and blessed them with the grace of Hari and Allah. This love of the common folk aroused jealousy among the priestly and Brahminic folk. It was therefore obvious that there was a latent opposition and friction in the people but the philanthropic and humanitarian divinity of Baba was destined to succeed in the end. The orthodox minds in the society have always shown an antipathy to higher souls who strive for welfare and upliftment of common man. On the contrary, pure, pious and moral sections of the society are attracted to the great Masters on account of their love and affection for suffering souls on this mundane earth. In the later segment of years from 1870 to 1878, people entertained a mixed reaction to the saintly fakir. Some called him a madman. Materialistic men like grocers ridiculed his ways of behaviour, whereas poor but pious men of faith loved him tenderly, respected him like a godman and followed him even through rough pathways in areas surrounding the village. The attitude of people did not disturb Baba's peace of mind, his tranquillity of soul, and the flow of divine love and grace came down on the ailing, suffering members of society who turned their face towards him for succour, help and relief. In these later years, Baba helped those who approached him with humanitarian love and compassion, blessed them and raised a ray of hope in the lives of the dejected. He gave medicines to the sick, warded off evils of those who suffered. In spite of this, the rustic village folk understood only little of the real glory and greatness of Sai Baba and his mission. The habitation in this forest-encircled area was made of small grass huts, the earthen houses of poor farmers and the roofed structures of well-to-do men who were rare. It was therefore that this fakir who performed miraculous acts and behaved eccentrically was taken to be a capricious aulia. His high profile as an ocean of compassion and love, incarnated splendour of the Supreme Brahma was very difficult to be realized by the village folk at this juncture. They had to be prepared gradually. This preparation was made when threads of Baba's divinity slowly unfolded.

The Initial Comrades and Colleagues in Shirdi

The Khandoba Temple provided Baba with his first followers whom he came across within the precincts of Khandoba shrine. The first and the foremost was the priest of the temple, who was a goldsmith by profession. The next ranking sadhus like Devidas and Jankidas were lovers of satsang and had been eager to receive sadhus, sanyasis, pilgrims and mendicants who happened to pass by Shirdi on the way to visit holy places in the North and South. These two holy men, also Mhalsapathi, Shimpi and Appa Jagle used to join these holy souls in welcoming and feeding the pilgrims, and hear words of wisdom from their mouth. Thus, they desired ardently to lift their souls to spiritual heights through *satsang* (group worship) and *upadesh* (sermon). Mhalsapathi was a poor man and could not provide help to the mendicant sadhus by himself. He compensated his inability to give money by rendering physical attention and service to the sadhus. Kashiram and Appa used to join Mhalsapathi in his service. They did whatever they could with their limited resources, when the pious men came to Khandoba Temple for darshan or for a momentary repose. These personalities held Baba in the highest esteem, treated him like demi-god. They saw through Baba's eccentric behaviour and realized that he was a great mahatma of very high spiritual order. Baba's capricious articulations, gestures, his waves of fury and wrath were ignored and tolerated by these early devotees. They did realize beyond his external appearance that he was a divine and renounced yogi of the level of a Guru. They showered their love and regard on Baba. Devidas and Jankidas also appreciated the colossal greatness of Baba's soul and tried their best to settle him in the hamlet of Shirdi. Many times Baba used to visit Neemgaon and Rahata (neighbouring towns). He loved the evolved householders like Babasaheb and Nanasaheb Dengle who were the first educated devotees to know and appreciate the young saint. He used to visit Chandrabhan Seth and Khushalchand Seth and inquire about their health and well-being. Thus, after several years of penance under the neem tree and in the Shirdi forest area, Baba changed his place of stay and daily routine.

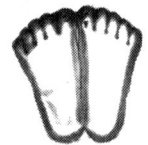

8

Baba Settles in Masjid (1870–80)

As most biographers of Baba have not portrayed his life story in chronological order, a reader fails to understand the stream of time and the flow of the saint's life during earlier days. Here we endeavour to unfold Baba's life beyond 1870 in a more consistent and logically ordered sequence.

Twelve Years of Penance (*Tapasya*)

We have seen how Baijabai's motherly love had a strong impact on Sai Baba's life prior to 1870. We have also seen how Devidas and Jankidas surrounded Baba for his satsang; how Kashiram, Appa and Mhalsapathi adored Baba in their simple rustic ways. After 1870, Baba finished his austerities and irregular life in the forest and under the neem tree and decided to settle somewhere in the village of Shirdi, as desired by his devoted followers. His life centred round the dilapidated mosque. His kafani cloth round the head, the tinpot in his hand and the *sataka* (staff) were his symbols. Going to Lendi Baug, merging in Shanti in Tapovan, growing marigold and rose plants in raw earthen pots near Gurusthan and watering them, remaining for a while with the people who approached him for their welfare, begging for alms from five selected houses was now his new way of living. He used to accept nothing else but onion, jawar bread and zunka, even when in later period offerings from his visitors flooded in.

Post-1870, Routine Life in Mosque

The impact of Kote Patil's family, viz. Ganpatrao and Bajabai remained unchanged in the post-1870 period as well. The Kote couple treated Baba as their family deity. He was a sage and a master to them. His service was held by them as a means to uplift them in both material as well as religious life. The farmers, aboriginals, Harijans as well as Sonar, Shimpi, Bhil, Lohar castes men in the village came to his fold. They liked to put forth their weal and woe before Sai Baba and get his hand of help. The Muslim folk as well as the Hindu followers came to pay him respect in his new abode. Men of faith desired his darshan. Even those who thought he was a madman or an eccentric sadhu took interest in him, as they experienced some divinity in his love, rage, madness and eccentricities. But men of faith were still few. There was no masjid structure as such in Shirdi in good condition, so as to call it a regular worshipping place. He only selected a barren dilapidated spot with broken walls, which happened to be an ignored site of mosque of bygone days. Before settling on the spot, Baba once set out for begging and when he reached the Hanuman Temple, he made his usual eccentric gestures, looking at the sky, talking to some unseen power and thereafter he moved to the mosque site and declared that he would stay there as that was his Dwarkamai. The place was cleaned so that Baba could sit there. He tied a bell in the mosque and started the dhuni. Thus, the mosque site was turned into a mandir and the fire shrine reconciling all faiths in one place. Before this Baba did not sit at one place. He wandered from place to place. He sometimes sat under the neem tree or near the riverbed. He reposed in the thorny shrubs or in the dense jungle. But now he seemed to negotiate with this strange new place for his stay and worship. Formerly, nobody but Baijabai followed and fed him as he walked to ridged and inaccessible jungle pathways. Now he seemed to settle in the village locality tolerating some interference by a few devotees. He liked to appear in the public and offer his satsang to the devoted bhaktas. Nobody dared to suggest him earlier that he may live in an ashram or monastery. But now he reconciled with an odd site of a ruined masjid. Baba said that God is everywhere. He would operate and react with his devotees from this very place. Baba's colleagues cleaned the floor, removed the stones and the stone walls. Baba put an earthen plate, two earthen pots, a tinpot, a grinding wheel and an earthen lamp in the place and assured that he would live in this place hereafter. This was the Dwarka of Sai Krishna. Baba selected the pedestal of Krishna idol for his last repose in this very Shirdi where he led his avataric life for sixty years, helping, transforming, uplifting the humanity from the darkness of ignorance.

Baba's Beginning of Begging Life

Sai Baba used to beg for alms only from five selective houses. The first one was Baija mother's house. He accepted only onion, bread of jawar, chutni, kalvan and pithla (zunka). All other offerings he rejected. He did not stay or wait for long before any of the houses. Neither did he talk except with Baijabai whom he called 'my Mami'. Even when offerings of food came in plenty in later years, Baba's ways never changed. He subsisted on the begged food alone. He placed the *bhiksha* (alms) in the open to allow birds and dogs to eat a portion; whatever was left he consumed. Only Baba could do this great and exemplary act. Baba used to call men with love with such epithets as Dada, Bhau, Kaka, Mama, etc. When he called 'Mami, bhakar ghal,' Baijabai used to come quickly with her motherly affection to render the service. Many times, she called him inside and offered him milk. Baba sometimes accepted her motherly offering. He never allowed anyone else to be familiar with him. She often asked him about his parents, his original birthplace and other details. He replied that he had his own house, parents, but they were far off. The relationship of a renounced saint with such a faithful mother was indeed divine and unique.

Baba's Colleagues

We have earlier referred to the sadhus like loving Devidas and Jankidas who yearned for Baba's satsang. They tried to learn the words of wisdom and sadhana from the mouth of Baba. Mhalsapathi had religious faith in Baba. He was allowed by Baba to do his *puja* (worship) in the masjid after he had worshipped Khandoba and other village deities. Next was Nanasaheb Dengle of Neemgaon, who was allowed by Baba to anoint chandan paste on his forehead and offer pooja material. Dengle brothers were educated, influential, ardent and dhyani and were therefore loved by Baba. Babasaheb was gifted with grace of progeny by Baba, whereas Nanasaheb (his brother) was vouchsafed with the eternal manifested darshan of Vishnu, when he met Baba in the waterbed named Shivacha Nala (streamlet). To Dengle, Baba was Narayan reposed on Shesh serpent. Nanasaheb then exclaimed, 'You are verily Vishnu reposing on serpent bed. You are Madhava, Mukunda, Shyam Sundar with Vaijayanti garland in your neck and Kausthubha diamond on your bosom. Baba you are my Eternal Purusha, Shri Maha Vishnu.' (*Sai Geetayan*)

Meeting with Saints from Swami Samarth Fold

During these years, Baba was mostly surrounded by uneducated, simple-minded village folk. They had no parameters to judge such a colossal divinity as Baba, moving in ragged attire of a fakir, who outwardly seemed like a madman but was a great Master inside. He did not desire that common people should know his divinity in depth. Jankidas and Devidas could probe his siddhahood to some extent only. Mhalsapathi and Baija knew his greatness but their affection was more enthused with love and admiration than exact appreciation and knowledge. He used to be calm and peaceful at a given moment, and red with rage at the very next one. His speech was limited, cryptic and strange. Hence, nobody dared to approach him and breed familiarity. Advent of Shyama was not on horizon until 1880, and there was no real companion or comrade for Baba to express himself, freely and unassumingly. Baba however knew the heart, the intent and the level of everybody who came in his masjid precincts. The people of some understanding saw him as an occult figure—mute, denounced and divine but at the same time freaky, capricious, eccentric and unfathomable. The rustics called him a madman, making gestures in front of Hanuman Temple, urinating at public places, making strange expositions of his unpredictable moods. However, they thirsted for his blessings, his medicines, his guidance. Nobody had the audacity to talk against or defy him. In this pre-publicity life of Baba in Shirdi, a few men of spiritual knowledge approached him. They were Bidkar Maharaj (1873) and Anandanath Maharaj (1875) from Swami Samarth fold of Akkalkot, for Baba was known and respected in the Dattatreya lineage of Swamiji. Nobody knows about Bidkar's visit. But visit of Anandanath is recorded in his life story and the Gangagir Baba of Giri cult in later year (1880), when Baba was rightly assessed by them.

9

Visit of Anandanath and Gangagir

*T*he period beyond 1870 was summarily cultured for the knowledge of our readers. Let us now see some prominent figures shedding light of their individuality and penance on Sai Baba's divine stream of daily life in the Shirdi mosque.

After Baba settled in the old masjid, which he called Krishna's Dwarka, the new life of *bhiksha-vritti* (practice of begging for meals) began. The company of saintly persons like Jankidas and Devidas, loving mother like Baijabai, devotees like Mhalsapathi, Kashiram, men of learning and respect in society like Nanasaheb Dengle sustained even after 1870 and had major contribution in Baba's life till a comrade devotee like Shyama came in 1880 and Abdulla, Chandorkar, Ganu followed Shyama after a decade or so. This period was mostly marked by the visits of householder villagers like Kote Patil, Nandaram Marwadi, Dagdu Gayake and others.

Nanasaheb Dengle was one who could penetrate his sight into Baba's outside appearance and judged him as an incarnation of Bhagwan Vishnu or Dattatreya who was living in Shirdi in a dormant personality. His vision of Vishnu form of Baba is aptly portrayed in *Sai Geetayan*.

The Dedication of Kashiram Tailor

Kashiram was Baba's original follower. He met Baba near the Khandoba Temple on his advent to Shirdi village. His devotion for Baba was such that he could offer everything he earned through his profession as a tailor and his business of selling cloth to rich people on marriage or festival occasions. He desired that Baba should partake of his money for his day-to-day needs in the masjid. He prepared a green kafani and cap for Baba. He also provided wood for the dhuni. Mhalsapathi was comparatively poor and could render only physical service to Baba. Lest Kashiram Shimpi's desire to cater to Baba turn into ego, Baba gradually began to accept money from him. He took so much that soon Kashiram was left with no money. His earnings also went on declining day by day and he become poorer. Then he realized that he couldn't provide for the needs of a saint. On the contrary, it is only the God and his messenger saint who can provide means of livelihood to the devoted followers. Thus, his ego was shed. The change in his attitude reflected on his earnings and soon he regained his professional earnings to a considerable extent. This devotion and dedication towards Baba earned him a covetable death on the sacred day of Ekadashi after he had served Baba for five decades. Similar end was earned by Appa Jagle who was a colleague and comrade of Kashiram. Once Kashiram was attacked by Ramoshi dacoits while he was returning from the market with the earnings from his sale of clothes. The thieves divested money from him. But he refused to give them a small bundle of sugar which he used to scatter to the ants as an act of piety to small animals. The Ramoshi thugs injured him and snatched the packet out of his hands. Sai Baba came to know about this from his divine vision and, sitting in the mosque, wildly waved his sataka in the air and abused the dacoits. Meanwhile, Kashiram regained consciousness. He killed two dacoits with their own swords and the remaining fled away. The injured tailor was carried to Baba's mosque on a donkey's back. Baba cured him of his wounds and advised him not to have attachment for even sugar reserved for ants. The attachment for both money and material must fully vanish from the mind of a devotee serving and worshipping God and godman. Later, the Government rewarded Kashiram with a sword for the valour shown by him against the gang of dacoits. The real valour was latent in Baba's help which protected him and enthused him with energy and courage to defy the dacoits and come out victorious in the entire encounter!

The Devotion of Mhalsapathi, the Priest

Mhalsapathi's devotion and dedication to the saint of Shirdi was exemplary. He was the priest of the Khandoba Temple. He had little means of earning and his life was full of poverty, austerities and non-attachment to money and means. Baba developed his vairagya in his dire poverty. He never gave him money or helped improved his financial circumstances. He allowed Mhalsapathi to perform his pooja after he had worshipped all other village deities. In fact, Mhalsapathi got the first greatest sermon of equality of religions and unity of godheads from the mouth of Baba before the Khandoba Temple. His devotion was of a comrade (*sakhya*) bhakti as well as service (*dasya*) bhakti. He was made to abandon all lusts and lures to develop his own self. Mhalsapathi's dedication to Baba was unequalled. He used to sleep in the masjid with Baba. After the demise of his only son, Baba sent him back home to beget a child. It is recorded with faith that the same son was born in his family within a period of one year. Mhalsapathi protected Baba's body when he suffered a serious asthma attack and raised his soul to Brahmanda (celestial sphere) for three days and nights spell. This was in 1886. Mhalsapathi had singular impact on Baba's life until Shyama (the primary school teacher) took over the reigns from him in 1880. Mhalsapathi lived a long life of satsang and merits, and left his body on an auspicious day in ripe old age.

The Dhyana Bhakti of Nanasaheb Dengle

We have dwelt with Dengle in the earlier sequence. He was an Inamdar of Neemgaon (Jali) village near Shirdi. He owned some land in Shirdi as well. He was an educated and influential man in the area and was highly respected in Government circles. He was the first dhyani bhakta of Sai Baba, whose life was influenced by Baba with his love and grace right from 1870 until the end of the century. He used to meet Baba in the forests prior to 1870. He used to watch Baba at the Shiva's stream while he was absorbed in deep meditation. He was infatuated by the divine bliss and celestial ecstasy on Baba's face and desired to attain a similar state by his grace. Baba told him, 'Nana, this life is mortal. See the immortal atma, which is beyond mundane existence. The kith and kin are bubbles on the mayic waters of sansar. You have to break this transitory web of Maya and dedicate your mind, body and ego to the Lord. The attachment for money and material things must be forsaken. You should be attached to the Lord alone. You have to perform karmas without expectation for the fruit. You have to see the live existence of Saguna form of Lord reigning in the external worldly appearances. The world is full with the element "Vasudeva" alone.' (*Sai Geetayan*) Baba prepared Nana as Krishna trained his disciple Arjuna. It was through the good offices of Nanasaheb and Babasaheb Dengle that Circle Inspectors like Gopalrao Gund and Collectors, personal aides like Gadgil were attracted to Shirdi and Sai Baba. Such educated and influential devotees were rare and scarce in these early years in Shirdi. They laid down the basis of educated people who later appeared in Shirdi within next two decades. Hence, their stepping in Shirdi was quite significant and momentous in the history of Shirdi.

Coming of Bidkar Maharaj and Anandanath Maharaj to Shirdi

We have referred to the saints from Swami Samarth fold who knew about divinity and glory of Sai Baba. Bidkar Maharaj (who was known as Ramanand Bidkar Swami) visited Shirdi in 1873 when Baba was still unknown in his true glory to the rustic villagers. What Bidkar saw at Shirdi is little known to biographers as there is no record of their meeting or encounter anywhere. Another saint from Swami Samarth fold was Anandanath Maharaj who happened to come to Sawargaon, a village near Shirdi. He was a saint, an inspired poet and a visionary disciple of Swami. He did not visit Shirdi as the chief residents were not present there at the point of time. When Dagdu Gayake, Nandaram Marwadi and Kote Patil returned to Shirdi, they came to know about Ananadnathji and they hurried down to Sawargaon to invite him to pay his auspicious visit to Shirdi. Anandanath himself sat in a bullock-cart and came out of his own will to see Sai Baba who was at that time watering the rose and marigold plants which he grew near his Gurusthan. Baba and Anandanath saw each other in their own divine way. Anandanath then returned fully edified and illumined about this Shirdi incarnation. He found that Swami (his Guru) was not different from Sai Baba. When the village chief requested him to stay on at Shirdi, Anandanath frankly told him that Shirdi village does not require his visitation and stay any more as young Sadhu (Sai) had sanctified the soil of Shirdi by his divine presence. The village had been endowed with fortune and auspiciousness by the touch of great incarnation of Baba's order. Anandanath told the villagers, 'Sai Baba is a diamond. Though he is not well known and well appreciated by common folk, he is a paragon among saints. Nobody can understand his true glory. He is a diamond on the dung hill. An incarnation is moving in Shirdi. He will transform not only Shirdi but also the entire land by his glory and teachings. Swami himself has invested his dormant power in Sai to reform the entire world. Swami's divine power will be manifested through this doyen among saints within a few years.' These words of Anandanath were well received by Shirdi folk but soon forgotten! The stage was not yet set to appreciate a great incarnation in the initial years of his moulding and growth. Advent of Anandanath in 1875 was followed by coming of another saint of Giri Sampadaya, namely Gangagir Maharaj.

Gangagir Maharaj Visits Dwarkamai (1880)

Gangagir Maharaj was a stout athlete and a man of sinews in his younger days. He turned into a Keertankar and a religious propagator of the name cult due to his study of shastras and the devotional lore. He spread the importance of the name of God. He held weekly programmes of recitation of God's name in public

Visit of Anandanath and Gangagir

gatherings. He was active in Ahmednagar district and adjacent Marathi and Nizam state areas of Marathwada. He was invited to various places to bless the villagers by conducting weeks of name recitation (*nama saptah*) in their area, to render the area auspicious and free of rampant ill currents by the potency of Hari's name. Once he came to Shirdi and was greeted by Mhalsapathi and Shyama. Shyama was recently posted as a primary teacher in Shirdi and was a comrade of Sai Baba, with whom he shared tobacco and chillum every day. Hence, both Mhalsapathi and Shyama were the first persons to welcome Gangagir Maharaj. Baba was, as usual, adoring his Guru by watering the rose garden near the neem tree. Gangagir Maharaj noticed Baba's glory and his devotion for his departed Guru. He came to know the halo of illumination round Baba's face and Baba's great heritage of Nath, Sufi and Datta cult. He was enchanted by his sight and said, 'He is a great incarnation. He will fill this village, this land, this nation and this world with divine glory of the Lord. He is the Lord whose name is recited by devotees. It is therefore not necessary that a nama saptah be held in Shirdi.' Baba invited Gangagir to Dwarkamai to share chillum with him. Baba said, 'O Changdev Maharaj, O Vateshwar of Vatgaon! Come, come! You are welcome in Dwarkamai.' Mhalsapathi, Shyama and Gangagir tasted the divine smoke of Sai Baba's chillum. Another saint thus declared Baba's great spiritual height and his mission of uplifting humanity. During these earlier days, Baba was not properly assessed in his true glory. Hence, such realistic appreciations were rare but exemplary parameters of Baba's latent glory.

Shama's Advent and Miracle of Lights

We have dwelt upon the 1870 to 1880, a decade in Baba's life when his fame was only dimly visible. Baba had completed his twelve years of penance under the neem tree and had come to settle down in the old dilapidated mosque, which he called Dwarkamai. He had started his life of begging for alms and people had access to his masjid sojourn for satsang as well. We have delineated his daily life in the mosque and acquainted ourselves with his prominent colleagues and comrades. Now we will try to enliven certain incidence in this decade of his introduction.

In 1875, Anandanath came to see Baba at Shirdi. We have pictured this meeting of two great saints in the last sequence. Anandanath Maharaj had then said to Shirdi's leading personalities, 'Your village no longer requires grace of God. The incarnation of God has alighted on the soil of Shirdi. Sai Baba is a live icon of my Guru Swami Samarth of Akkalkot. He is not a sadhu or saint. He is the paragon of all saints and spiritual masters in the world. This Shirdi will now bathe in new fortune and new light.' These great words are recorded in cultural history of Shirdi village. In 1880, when Gangagir came face to face with Sai Baba, Baba invited him to share his chillum, along with Mhalsapathi the priest and Shyama, who had recently come to Shirdi. Gangagir Maharaj told the residents of Shirdi, while bidding farewell to them, 'Sai Baba's glory cannot be equalled with anybody. Shirdi will be a great place of pilgrim in few years. Shri Hari has himself descended on earth.'

As *Sai Geetayan* has described:

'The sun has appeared on the Shirdi horizon
This fakir is the royal harbing or the Majestic Sarkar
Of the city of liberation.'

Shyama's (Madhavrao Deshpande) Arrival

Nobody was so near and dear to Sai Baba as Shyama used to be. The primary school teacher's school overlooked the masjid. Baba used to speak loudly, make strange gestures, fly with rage, and beat those who acted wrongly. Shyama was at first very much scared of Baba's behaviour. He thought that Sai Baba was a madman. Soon he was attracted to Baba and shared his tobacco and chillum. He was more devoted to the chillum than to Baba initially. Later however his proximity to Baba transformed him. He left his classes of primary school and spent much of his time in the masjid in Baba's company. Shyama spoke to Baba so intimately that soon he became a middleman, guide and interpreter between the saint and visiting devotees from around the world. The intimacy of Shyama would reflect in Baba's life in the later years. Baba used to admonish Shyama, Baija, Kashiram, Ganpatrao, Mhalsapathi and Nanasaheb Dengle in simple words. The style of his upadesh was cryptic, concise and he gave his guidance to each according to his level, his need and his development. When people used to come, they would ask Shyama to receive any help and grace of Sai Baba. He became a *badwa* (middleman) of Sai Baba's Shirdi!

Upadesh to Each According to His Level

Shyama used to tell Baba, 'You are not such a God, who can give us all we want. You are the naughty God who gives us pinches.' Baba told him that he was related with Shyama for seventy-two generations but he (Baba) never harmed him. Shyama then said that Baba was a liar because his age was not equal to seventy-two generations. If he were indeed so old, he should tell Shyama whether the monkeys actually built a bridge on the sea, as described in the Ramayana. Baba swore by his life and told him that he would never lie before the dhuni. He was present during the Ramayana days and he saw the setu being built by the monkeys. Such were their friendly encounters. Shyama then asked Baba whether *deva lokas* (abodes of god) were genuine. Baba told him that these were the stations on the way to progress of *jivatma* (self). He and his devotees need not care for these locations, because he would lead his men by a different route of grace. Shyama little understood the greatness of Baba's words. For lack of knowledge could not judge the atma, its stages of development and grace of Guru. This was an example how Baba taught his own men. He asked Shyama to read *Vishnusahasranama* because of its potency of mantric value. The great principle Vasudev was behind the sahasranama (thousand names) and it would certainly end all his household as well as spiritual deficiencies by its own inherent power of bhakti and grace. Here, readers may see Baba's mild and graceful manner of talking to a comrade devotee who was attached to his physical person, and his knowledge was not of higher stature. God gives the fruits according to karma and destiny but saints interfere for their intimate devotees and make their sufferings mild and tolerable. Baba told Shyama that those devotees who forget themselves in recitation of his name and singing glory of his leelas are carried over the ocean of sansar. Baba has sworn this grace in the Dwarakamai in front of the dhuni and it was an eternal truth that Baba carried the burden of his devoted, dedicated and surrendered devotees in order to liberate them.

Baba did not impose heavy sadhanas upon his rustic devotees like Baija and Tatya. He told them that their satsang in the masjid was sufficient for their upliftment. He was fastened to them by the bond of love. He was their father and they were destined to earn everything from their love as Baba's children. It was the merit of past births that had brought them so nearer to the incarnation of liberation as Baba himself was! The demands of *artha* (material) and *artharthi* (demanding) devotees were fulfilled by Baba turning their mundane ignorance into advanced knowledge. In the Geeta, it is said that those who adore God will reach His abode. Mhalsapathi was poor, uneducated and a devotee of *archana* (prostration) or *vandana* (worship) bhakti. He was asked to worship and pray to all village godheads and lastly to worship Baba's feet. This gave him the opportunity of shedding his mortal coil in peace. The dedication and surrender of Appa and Kashiram earned them highest fruit of dying on an auspicious (Ekadashi) day and merging in Sai. Dengle brothers were dhyani and educated. Baba gave them the vision to see the form of God in every object, whether sentient or non-sentient. They were taught the selfless karma of Geeta. They were of higher spiritual stature. Hence, Baba taught them that the entire universe is filled with the principle *Vasudev* in Upanishad style. The Vasudev will relieve them from sansar and lead them to spiritual peace and tranquillity. This was universal merger of dhyani.

Swami Samarth's Samadhi and the Miracle of Lights

Swami Samartha left his avataric body in 1878. He had earlier indicated that, hence forward, he would operate through Shirdi Sai Baba. In every age, the immortal power of Guru manifests through great sages. After the departure of Akkalkot incarnation, the power decided to manifest through the secular and humanitarian incarnation of Sai, which had appeared on the earth to unite all religion sects, castes and creeds and to preach unity of godheads and the divinity of Swami Samarth. The saint of Shirdi was silent until these days. Baba's first great miracle was broadcast through the great miracle of lights, where Baba burnt oil lamps using water to keep the masjid lit.

Miracle of Lights

The Almighty decided to manifest his glory through Shirdi village to outside areas of Maharashtra. Ahmednagar, Pune, Marathwada and Vidarbha areas were rich with devotion for saintly persons. The glory of Baba remained unnoticed until he turned forty-five in 1880. It was after the samadhi of Swami Samartha that the glory of Baba slowly manifested beyond the boundaries of Shirdi village. Sai Baba started begging for alms in two selected houses in Shirdi when he settled in the Dwarkamai in 1870. He had a strange habit of begging for oil in order to light the masjid with lamps. The masjid was the abode of his Guru and Baba was an advocate of the path of light (*prakash marg*). Once the merchants in Shirdi refused to dole out oil for him as they thought it was a luxury wasted on a madman. Baba was not disheartened by the folly of the unwise merchants. He drank some water from his tinpot and filled the earthen lamps with the residual water. He turned water principle into fire principle by offering it to the *atmaram* (god). He kindled fire and lighted lamp after lamp in Dwarkamai. The lamps burnt in the mosque incessantly until morning. The entire village was amazed by the strange happening, the miracle of miracles that occurred in front of their own naked eye. This was the first miracle which Baba manifested in order to illumine the splendour of his path of light to the ignorant humanity.

Sai Geetayan Describes

'The wicks burnt without oil. When the lustre of the soul is illumined, even the earthen lamps burn without oil. This is the miraculous way of the Lord of the Universe.' The glory of Sai Baba spread from the village huts and the houses to far-off villages, from villages to the towns in Ahmednagar district, from Nagar district to cities like Pune, Bombay, Nagpur and Aurangabad. A new horizon of understanding was opened for all educated, uneducated, rustic and ignorant. The light of the atma dazzled to signify that the universal light has descended on earth. Until this time, Sai fame was limited to urban and rural Maharashtra only.

Morning of Baba's Sainthood (1880–90)

*L*et us now switch over to the comparatively visible years (1880–90) of Baba's life, i.e. the decade following his first great miracle of lighting lamps with water. The approach of Shirdi village and the knowledgeable persons in adjacent villages and towns nearby became more realistic and deeper with greater insight into his occult divinity.

The Light of Morning

People realized that some great siddha power resided in the frail little frame of the fakir of Shirdi. The villagers looked at Baba with more curiosity and respect. Educated people like Dengle brothers and others could also gather more respect for the strange, unique fakir. People came to the mosque to hear great life truths and philosophy from the obscure and tacit phrases emanating from the lips of the fakir. Baijabai, Ganpatrao Kote Patil, Mhalsapathi, and new rising comrades like Shyama, Kashiram, Appa and Dagdu Gaike were normal visitors to the mosque. Villagers of Muslim faith also came to listen to the aulia Sai Baba. There was still a decade before Chandorkar and Ganu, the propagators of the new Shirdi precepts, would appear in Shirdi. The brighter half of Baba's life was yet to come.

Readers must clearly see this distinction of time, period and personalities against the saint's glory, because other biographies have mixed the events and chronology to the maximum extent.

Shyama

We have earlier mentioned the advent of the great devotee and comrade of Baba, Shyama, who was initially attracted to Baba for his chillum sessions rather than for the spiritual faith. He came to Shirdi between 1880 and 1885, and was established as a comrade in the mosque by 1885–90. He became a permanent sakha of Baba in later period and outlived Baba, with his precious memories stored in the mind. He realized that he could not judge Sai's glory and divinity even after a longer companionship with him in the sacred Dwarkamai. The dynamic devotees during the decade 1880 to 1890 were Mhalsapathi, Kote Patil, Dengle, Appa Jagle, Shyama, Jankidas and Devidas. Mhalsapathi, Tatya and Shyama slept with Baba in the Dwarkamai on each alternate day, whereas Jankidas, Devidas and new visitors of religious faiths used to stay at Chawdi, the meeting place of village folk. On other days Baba slept in Chawdi for the benefit of other bhaktas. This convention of sleeping in Chawdi and mosque was followed by Baba regularly.

Avoid Debt, Enmity and Violence (1885)

We are aware how Baba used to teach each one according to his level and eligibility to receive divine guidance from his mouth. Baba had asked Baija and Ganpatrao to treat him as their father and demand everything from him. He was teaching absolute surrender to the Guru in this way. To Mhalsapathi, he taught worshipping with devotion. Puja of village deities and thereafter doing service to Baba was the way to his liberation. To Shyama, Baba asked to recite *Vishnusahasranama*. To Nanasaheb Dengle, Baba vouchsafed vision of Narayan and taught him the balance of dhyana bhakti like that of Arjuna, whereby he can renounce greed or attachment and do selfless duty to kith and kin by acting in a fixed and poised state of mind of the dhyani. He taught each person what he most needed and what he actually deserved. To rustic people and the villagers, he illustrated life of piety and morality that is free from lust and lure, through suggestive and symbolic events or happenings for they could understand by examples alone. Once Baba was sitting on the edge of a village brook waiting for some happening, when a wayfarer approached him. Baba offered his chillum to the passerby. This was in 1885. Suddenly they heard a shriek and an agonized cry for help. Baba said, 'See, Veerbhadrappa is swallowing poor Basappa!' The stranger was wonderstruck. When they approached the scene of agony, they saw the frog (Basappa of past birth) being swallowed by a serpent (Veerbhadrappa of previous birth). Baba explained, 'Man has to reap the fruits of his past karmas. Lust for land and money had degenerated those two human beings into animals. Yet they have not forsaken their enmity. The debt, enmity and violence are to be repaid. I promised Basappa that I would save him from death in his animal birth. So I have been waiting here for the duel to begin on the bank of the stream.' He called loudly to the serpent in a warning cry and made him drop the frog, saying, 'Are you not ashamed to carry the enmity to a new birth? Act wisely.' The serpent obeyed Baba's order and slipped into the bushes, never to be seen again. The wayfarer was so wonderstruck that he fell on the feet of Baba and went home. Baba always preached by simpler events and examples. Not only his words, the entire world was a blackboard for Baba to teach his devotees and impart to them practical demonstrations with lessons of morality.

The Recitation of Name in Dwarkamai (1885)

All four companions, Mhalsapathi, Tatya, Shyama and Baba used to discuss various topics during their stay in the mosque at night. Baba used to enlighten and edify them on material as well as spiritual matters. They were the true comrades and playmates of Sai Baba during these years. When Baba slept in the mosque, the name of Rama echoed in all the limbs of his body. He used to ask all of them to listen to the recitation by putting their ears against his hands, feet and heart. He had asked them to rouse him from sleep if the recitation stopped abruptly. But it never stopped. The three snored in sleep but the name continuously resounded in Baba's heart. The name Rama came to Baba since he was Kabir, initiated in Rama's name by Saint Ramanand of Kashi. The incessant *japa* (recitation of name) joined Baba to the Soham (Ajapajapa) of Natha cult. Rama became Soham and Soham merged in Om. Baba's name was coupled by his dhyana or meditation in the form of Guru. The 'name' is recitation but 'smarana' stands for the dwelling on Guru's form. Both are essential for sadhana. The name potent with Guru's power becomes subtle sound and enters into higher planes of existence. The form or the roopa becomes Atmic light or flame and merges beyond the crest point into universal awareness. The name also, after becoming Nada, enters crest point and merges into cosmic awareness. These sadhanas, although sound apart, are similar or identical and lead to one and the same realization of self and merger with cosmic God (Guru Deva). The difference and symbolic importance of these sadhanas were not explicit to those old bhaktas in the old Dwarkamai. But Baba is now rising up to make the devotee realize his Guruhood and also Guru charitra through these significant pages. We are very fortunate today to write down, explain and understand the essence of Baba's teaching about sadhana. Baba laid more stress on roopa in this birth as in Guru Geeta. He said, 'You look up to me and I shall look at you.' This deeksha or initiation of Guru looking into the heart of disciple was sufficient to Baba. 'Dhyanamoolam Gurormurti' was his command as per ancient Guru Geeta. There was directness and personal touch embedded in this form of Guru dhyana.

Miracle of Plank (1890)

Dengle brothers were regular visitors to the mosque. Sai Baba used to sleep in the mosque on a gunny bag every alternate night. Usually dust particles and waste material covered the masjid ground. Dengle was pained to see Sai sleeping soundly in such state and decided to bring a jackfruit plank from Neemgaon for Baba to sleep on. The plank was heavy and strong. Baba tied the plank to the roof of the masjid with ropes made of rags of his kafanis. The rags were so old and feeble it seemed they could hardly support such a heavy plank. Baba kept four lighted lamps on the four corners of the plank and slept soundly on it at night. Amazingly, nobody ever saw Baba climb the plank, nor saw him alight from it. It was a mystery for all. A great miracle, only second to the lighting of lamps with water instead of oil! This miracle exhibited Sai Baba's eight maha siddhis (powers). When Madhavrao

(Shyama) asked Baba how he climbed or got down the plank, Baba smilingly told him that all directions, all ups and downs were one and the same to him. He was indeed beyond directions, time and space. The devotees asked whether this could be possible for them to do, Baba said that the name of Rama was incessantly resounding in his veins. If they could do it too, the siddhi will be a possibility, for siddhis are fruits or rewards of self-control and penance. But Baba was keen that common man should not be allured by the powers. He saw many people coming to mosque to see the plank tied to roof by rags and express their curiosity. Baba was highly disturbed by the exhibition and, in a fit of rage, broke the plank and dismantled the infrastructure of plank miracle.

Abdulla, the First Muslim Disciple Appears in Shirdi (1890)

After Mhalsapathi and Shyama, a third disciple-cum-devotee appeared on the scene of Dwarkamai. He was a Muslim youth of nineteen years. There were no Muslim followers worth the name prior to this. This man came from the Marathwada town of Nanded, where his Guru Amruddin Fakir lived. Baba gave a vivid vision to this fakir and told him to send his disciple to Shirdi. Baba invited Abdulla and accordingly the latter appeared in Shirdi at the command of his Guru. Baba welcomed Abdulla by calling him, 'My crow has come.' He was a sweeper, server of the masjid, a *halalkhor* (faithful) who fetched and stored drinking water in the Dwarkamai. He followed his Muslim rituals and mixed among the Hindu devotees most amicably. He earned love from all and grace from Sai Baba. He was allowed to record and preserve words of wisdom and upadesh coming out of Sai Baba's lips. He outlived Baba and fulfilled his life mission as a genuine follower of Sai Baba. Baba made him see the 'sun and moon in his own body'. He was a great addition to Sai family in 1890, a little prior to the bright period commencing later in 1890–1900, when Ganu and Chandorkar stepped in.

12

Baba's Begging Round

The First Part of Baba's Unknown or Partially Known Life Ends Here (1880–90)

We have recorded the coming of young Muslim aspirant Abdulla to Shirdi during 1890 in the last chapter. He became a part of Sai's life due to his service, dedication and Baba's upadesh to him. The illumination of the two major miracles, namely lighting of lamps with water and sleeping on a heavy plank fixed to the ceiling by torn rags was still fresh in the memory of Shirdi and adjacent village folk. The first half of Baba's life (1835–90) comes to an interval by way of pause here. The later half (1890–1900) begins with the advent of Nanasaheb Chandorkar and Das Ganu Maharaj who were first introduced to Baba between 1892 and 1895. Later they became the propagators of Baba's *mahima* (glory) to people of Maharashtra and conscious cities like Bombay, Pune and adjacent areas. This is crucial period whereafter Baba manifested himself in manifold dimensions of his sainthood which remained undiscovered so far.

We have portrayed the astounding way of Baba's slumber in the Dwarkamai, as if he was Lord Dattatreya sleeping among the tunes of lullaby sung by the eight maha siddhis. This was a great miracle eloquent of the colossal prowess of the Master sitting as a common fakir dressed in rags. The advent of Abdulla was the appearance of another apostle of Baba only next to Mhalsapathi, the dedicated pujari of Khandoba, and Shyama, the comrade and lively colleague of Baba in his day-to-day masjid life. However, these could not be compared with the dhyani devotee, Nanasaheb Dengle, for his understanding, education and status in contemporary society was much higher. Abdulla followed the Muslim way of life and sadhana but mixed freely with the Hindu devotees and slowly became part and parcel of Baba's daily routine. We have to now make our readers visualize Baba's living on alms got from select five houses in Shirdi, his use of ashes or udi as a blessing to his devotees, which was deeply meaningful as an instrument of his divine mission.

The Lord Begs for Alms in Shirdi

Sai Baba, after finishing his roving life, came to settle in the mosque between 1870 and 1880. In this decade as well as subsequent decades, Baba and the Dwarkamai masjid became synonymous. His Guru lying under the neem had come to stay with him in the Dwarkamai. He was a Sufi master, the Fakir, the Trinity or Lord Datta, who directed Baba to act and speak, and Baba simply obeyed his dictates. The fakir was the Malang form of the Supreme Gururaj. He begged for bread from five select village houses as per the command of his Guru. This was his vow of living on alms. But what was the propriety of Baba's begging when Laxmi was at his sacred feet? He was Lord of Laxmi! However, he used to spread his *jholi* (edge of cloth) and ask the village housewives to lend a loaf of bread and the ladies quickly responded. Sometimes they served him bread with chilli chutney or onion. He used to move barefooted in the hot sun of the noontime. He blessed the village mothers. The ladies knew that the renounced saints have to subsist on begged food, for they cannot cook food as per vowed rules. Whatever he collected, Baba kept on an earthen plate for crows, dogs and other animals to share and subsisted on the remains alone. He used to eat from the mouth of all. His hunger was quenched when others were happy and satisfied. He was the Lord and the Lord set out to beg! A strange paradox indeed! *Sai Geetayan* describes it as follows:

> 'A strange thing occurs on the earth
> The Lord has set out to beg for food.'

This was the majesty of Baba's begging. He was the most compassionate and liberal-hearted Swami of the three worlds. He had no wants. Dengle was surprised to see the begging scene. He thought that the Goddess Laxmi herself is begging in the ragged fakir attire of Sai Baba. Mhalsapathi was sure that Baba could obliterate the line of destiny on a man's forehead and inscribe a totally new fate as a substitute. Baba was the wish-fulfilling tree; he was the kamadhenu (miracle cow), the diamond called chitamani himself. Then why was he begging? He was the fortune of Shirdi residents standing at their door. He was the Lord of destiny, Master of fate calling at each village door. He was indeed not begging! He was searching the hearts of Shirdi people!

Sai Geetayan says:

> 'Is he bothered about a loaf of bread?
> He is searching the recesses of our hearts!'

This golden moment is of great value. The fortune of Lord coming to your door and asking for something will never occur in your life again. This dramatic event moved the hearts of Shyama, Mhalsapathi and Dengle. Baba does not want flower, fruit, water or leaf. He does not pine for bread; he wants you to offer your mind, body, intellect and ego at his feet. He wants dedication and surrender. He wants total merger. This is a simple but practical lesson.

The Ashes from Dhuni, the Divine Blessing from Baba

The other significant thing attached with Baba's life was the ash obtained from the dhuni, which he offered to the devotees. It was a miraculous offering of the Dwarkamai, which was the universal mother. The use of udi was a substitute for the medicines Baba formerly gave to his ailing devotees. Baba, when he started living in the mosque, became a physician for poor village folk whom he gave medicines for cure. But one day he stopped the medical treatment and started giving only udi saying, 'Hari, Hari.' The recitation of the name of Hari gave him the power to meet Lord Hari in person and the ashes became the link with the grace of Shri Hari. The udi turned into medicine and cured the patients.

Though the udi was originally a medicine for ailing, it became a medicine for the *bhava roga* (the agony of sansar). It has the grace of Lord and it operated in many ways. First, it was blessing. Secondly, it was medical aid. Thirdly, udi became the symbol of love of Hari. The ashes ultimately became *raksha-bandhan* (talisman for protection) for the devotees. It was the amrita or *sanjeevani* (the paneccia). *Sai Geetayan* described the holy ashes thus:

> 'The ashes in the burning dhuni in Dwarkamai
> decree the fate of human existence.
> For the ashes are the end product of the body made of a
> message of mortality to the persons steeped
> in sansar. Equally ashes are symbol of immortality of soul
> to those who are pious, spiritual and lovers of God.'

The ashes show that the material life of lusts and lures is transitory, illusory and momentary. For those who follow higher spiritual values, the ashes are pointers to the divine music of immortal life beyond physical death. Ashes were sacred, auspicious, protective, a token of divine compassion and ambrosial grace of God. 'Anoint that ash to your forehead for it is the vision of divine life beyond the mundane existence on this planet of earth. There is a celestial light behind the sansar. The ashes open the door to the gateway of the life of immortality. The ashes are the bond of love of the Master of Dwarkamai (Sai Baba) with his devout followers.' *Sai Geetayan* has brought home this point most effectively.

> 'The udi is the magic of the masjid!
> It is the alchemy of Allah the Master!
> It is the divinity and compassion of fakir.
> It is the tie of love bound by Lord of Vaikuntha.'

(Sai Geetayan)

The magical experiences of the grace inherent in ashes are already stored in the heart of the devotees and hence, we will not enumerate such great illustrations. After dwelling upon the main features of Baba's life (beyond 1870) within the precincts of the Dwarkamai, we will finish this first half of Baba's charitra. This first half of Baba's life was not visible during 1835 to 1858; it became dimly visible after 1870. The effort of the author is to throw spotlight on this unknown or partially known life of the Shirdi saint. The devotees were vouchsafed visions of Shiva, Vishnu, Devi, Rama and Krishna by Baba during these years to cater to their faith and consolidate their belief in the devotional endeavour. But who was Sai Baba? He was the multi-formed Guru.

Sai Baba Is Dwarkapati Vishnu

The readers already know that Sai Baba had vouchsafed the vision of Sheshashayi (serpent-couched) Lord Narayana to Nanasaheb Dengle who used to attend to him near Shiva's brook near Neemgaon, an adjacent place to Shirdi. The Dengle family was faithful and loved Baba as their Guru and guide. Nanasaheb especially was a dhyani bhakta who liked to observe the meditative face of Sai Baba. This gave him immense joy and peace of mind. He took Baba to be Lord Vishnu (or Krishna) as he was living in Dwarkamai. Dengle was so spellbound by the darshan of Lord Vishnu, that he exclaimed, 'He is Narayana with conch and discus and sleeping on the bed of Serpent Shesha. He is Madhav, Mukund, Keshav, Suresh, Shri Hari.' He had no words to describe the great divine celestial form of Sai Baba, the resident of Dwarkamai. In fact, Baba was the resident of Vaikuntha Loka of Vishnu. He was enthroned on the seat of heart of devout bhaktas. In fact, Rama, Krishna, Shiva, Hanuman, Devi, etc. were not the real forms of Baba. He was Lord Dattatreya, the master of Laxmi, Shripad Shri Vallabha incarnated for uplifting and liberating his bhaktas. In the form of Guru, the supreme Trinity, all forms are herein. All forms emanate from this Sanathan form and ultimately merge to Dattatreya form. Baba was Brahma, he was also Vishnu and Shiva. He was the Tripurasundari, the ultimate power of Lord creating, sustaining and destroying all universe.

Sai Geetayan says:

'Sometime he looks like Shiva, sometimes as Vishnu. But he is Shripad Shri Vallabha (Guru form) which is universal principle working for human upliftment.'

13

Baba Rejoins His Universal Mission

*I*n the earlier chapter of this book, we have covered the dusky years (1835–90) of Baba's life. These constitute forty-five years of Baba's bodily existence on earth. We have analysed these years with the eyes of faith as well as critical scanning. We have viewed these years with poetical symbolism as well as practical reasoning. We are entering now into the second half of Baba's comparatively known and revealed years of life (1890 to 1918). The later half of Baba's life was resplendent with visitation of true, knowledgeable devotees, men of letters, officers, writers, poets, professors and persons from various occupations. These personalities provided a worthy framework to Baba's divine glory. This later half ushered Baba's avatarhood to light. We wish to throw some more light on this period. Baba's glorious Guruhood shines apart from both these hemispheres and will be rediscovered and projected.

The Interval

The intervening period between the two hemispheres of Baba's life has been described by us in the earlier chapters. Baba's lively image as an incarnation uniting all Indian religious thoughts, concepts about godheads and the differences in human life, and caste/creed gradations, his teaching a new religion of unity, equality and humanitarian outlook did not fully emerge in these earlier years, when he was seen as an eccentric madman or a capricious godman. A few saints had assessed his greatness and few men of insight had appreciated his mission but to a large multitude of men of practical outlook, his individuality was doubtful and mysterious. However, Hindus and Muslims thronged around him to receive his grace and blessings and derive benefits from his benevolent powers. He wanted both Hindus and Muslims to adore him freely in their own way. But Dwarkamai, being a mosque, created religious hurdles, frictions and jealousies in conflicting communities in the hamlet. Although people were leading life in general understanding and amity, formal differences were rising up from the outward surface. These dents, in fact, were caused by contradictions in religious beliefs and rituals. Hindu bhaktas used *kumkum* (vermilion powder), *akshata* (yellow rice for worshipping) and sandal paste (*chandan*) on Baba's forehead, to which Muslims would object. *Bhajans* (religious songs), *artis* (pujas), sounding of drums, cymbals and uproar in the mosque were very unpalatable and provocative to the Muslim faith. Muslims viewed Baba as an Islamic saint, reading the Quran Sharif and following namaz practices. His declaration that 'Everything is Allah', 'Nothing is greater or higher than Allah', echoed dictates from the Quranic beliefs. Baba had to cater to both faiths equally. When anointment of chandan to Baba's forehead and puja was objected to by Muslims, Baba intervened and accepted Mhalsapathi's puja and Dengle's ritualistic adoration. Soon after 1890, the Hindu bhaktas outnumbered Muslims and the pujas were a common scene. Although Baba's Nath, Kabir and Sufi cult opposed idol worship and rituals, Baba could not put away obstinate Hindu devotees and gradually allowed their worship. After 1900, the pomp of arti rath (chariot), palanquin processions, umbrellas, chamaras and other rituals took luxurious propagations and Baba reluctantly allowed them in the mosque and its surroundings in Shirdi. Baba's namaz was short and symbolic. He taught the Quran to Abdulla and Geeta to Chandorkar in later years. But Baba's compromise to the various faiths was full of understanding and tolerance. He was an unattached, unritualistic *sanyasi* living by begging for alms, sleeping on a gunny cloth and wearing torn kafani. In later years, even when he asked for dakshina, he distributed everything to his wanting and deserving devotees, keeping nothing for himself. When he took samadhi in 1918, he had only Rs 16 and a few earthen pots and torn clothes with him. The outer pomp and Sagunopasana thrusted by the bhaktas upon him did not affect or change his inner core. When Muslims objected to performance of Hindu rituals in the mosque, Baba reconciled them that Islam does not lose anything if other faiths worship him in his abode (mosque). They should be tolerant. Even in earlier days in the mosque, Baba sent flowers from the Gurusthan to Muslim tombs as well as Hindu temples and shrines. Baba showed his humility in earlier days by accepting the Guruhood of Jawar Ali (Maulana) until he was exposed by Devidas and Jankidas in a debate and expelled from Shirdi. Baba was a rare mixture of all faiths and he knew the heart of all religions and spiritual aspirations of the Indian public. He disregarded external exposition of their outcomes. He understood the simple heart, the benign faith, the depth of sentiments, the immense love for God and longing for compassion to the humanity as a whole.

Personal God

The need for adoration of a personal God or a divine personality is an essential characteristic of Indian spiritualism. The love for idol worship has its seeds in this age-old attitude or approach. Even Muslims worship their aulias, saints or murshid (Guru) in a similar fashion, even though they are averse to idol worship. Baba's spirituality was highly unconditioned or nirguna. However, in order to attract people and harness them to a common, tolerant and compromising religious view, it was inevitable that a mystic saintly godhead was worshipped and followed as a 'Guru or God'. Since the beginning, up to 1886, Baba's secular attitude was natural and benign. It was derived from his Kabir birth. He tried to adjust his Hindu and Muslim followers with his duel signs of Hinduism and Islamic faith. This reconciliation was a part of the campaign of Akbar's short-lived efforts, Kabir and Guru Nanak's attempts to bring the jarring and warring religions and sects on a common humanitarian platform. Kabir's acidic opposition to idol worship, rituals and orthodoxy and upholding unconditioned mysticism was more broad-based. However, it ended with his life and his followers were divided, weakening the movement. Nanak's followers also did not take serious note of uniting factions among religions. This last movement of unity of God, equality of man and harmony among religions was to be taken in full velocity by a new godman and mystic. Baba realized this by 1886, when he declared that he would go to Allah's abode for a few days. He had been ordained by Allah himself to carry on the great mission on his powerful almighty shoulders because no other mystic had the power and glory of divinity to lift this great bow of Shiva. It was Baba alone destined to undertake this onerous task of uniting humanity in the fold of love and compassion. The second phase of Baba's life (1890–1918) was clearly a landmark of a new mission as an avatar.

Baba's New Mission

The intelligent readers would understand the avataric change in Baba's life, which turned him into a Guru and a missionary of the stature of a divine and all-powerful godman, i.e. the Sai Baba, as we know him today in wider connotation. Baba, therefore, attracted great devotees like Das Ganu, Chandorkar, Upasani, Sathe, Dixit, Khaparde, Dabholkar, Meher Baba, Narasimha Swamiji and many others to his circle of devotees. The later half of Baba's life thus gains in progressive light of illumination, expansion and upliftment coupled with his individual grace and succour to common devotees as well. At one side he rose in stature as Guru and godman to edify and uplift both materialistic and spiritual men, and at the other end he laid a strong foundation for a philosophy of unity of godhead, equality of mankind, harmony of religions and a need to direct life to love, compassion and service, so that the entire humanity made of individuals rises upto piety, morality, self upliftment and salvation.

14

Arrival of Abdulla and Chandorkar

The later half of Sai Story stands unveiled from the last chapter wherein we have pictured how Baba left for Allah's abode in 1886 and how Mhalsapathi protected his body for three days and three nights until he was sent back by the Lord with a mission of uniting and uplifting human race with a wider universal latitude as compared to his earlier birth as Kabir. Kabir's uniting of godheads, uniting humanity on a platform of equality and equity, deviating from the dividing religion of sects, rigours and orthodoxy stands revived at this turn of events. He had to bear the flag of Kabir and Nanak on his shoulders and widen it to universality befitting to this age of frictions and factions. He decided from 1890 until his samadhi to launch a new outlook based on his universal personality and stellar Gurupower. He attracted and collected bhaktas from different quarters, including distressed, destitutes as well as dhyanis, yogis and educated and evolved men of vision and capability. A wider approach of universal sainthood opens out here.

The revolutionary transformation in Baba's working style and objectives, which marked the later years of his life since 1886, is to be seen and appreciated in true spirit to know his journey from siddhahood to avatarhood, from saintly existence to Satchitananda—Satguru status. His individuality, glory and mission assumed enormous proportions in these days. The creeper of his mahima rose to celestial heights, embracing the universal Guruhood. This is the significance of a new era, which sprouts from this juncture in Sai Baba's life story.

Abdulla and Chandorkar's Place in the Framework

Two significant events took place in 1890 and 1892. Sai Baba, by his divine power and vision, attracted Muslim follower Abdulla to his fold and propelled Chitnis to Ahmednagar District Collector (namely Nana alias Narayan Chandorkar) to his expanding spiritual circle. Abdulla was a concrete example of a Muslim way, an aspirant living in amity with Hindu followers of Sai Baba, although following his own style of godward journey without interruption or interception. Though Islamic faith followers of Baba were limited in number and shallow in faith, Abdulla was the most loyal and tenacious aspirant whose behaviour and attitude towards people of other faiths was tolerant and liberal. He would be an open demonstration of piety, faith and service to other Muslims in Shirdi or visitors who arrived to meet Baba. Chandorkar was educated, learned, pious, morally sound and a devoted Hindu aspirant balancing Government duty, Hindu household life and sadhana in accordance with teachings of scriptures like Geeta and Bhagwat. His arrival was immediately following Abdulla's advent. Das Ganu, the famous *tamasha* (form of entertainment) and *lavani* (form of song) writer and poet, who was Nana's police guard, arrived in Shirdi with Nana. But he was then without any faith or attachment for Baba. With the grace of Baba, later he developed into a bard of Sai Baba's glory. Sai Baba had to mould, remould and develop both Nana and Ganu in his own unique and miraculous way of teaching by visions, experiences, events and with realities of life to which he exposed them. Ganu and Nana became the propagators of Sai Baba's divine mission in Pune, Bombay and Maharashtra. These three covered a period of fifteen years from 1890 to 1905 with their influence on public and grace of Baba until Sathe, Dixit, Bhishma, Kushabhau and Upasani enlightened the circles of educated and dhyani devotees by their arrival and presence after 1905.

Abdulla and Muslim Way of Sadhana Life

Baba had caused a vision to Amruddin Fakir of Nanded and made him send Abdulla to Shirdi. He was a dear child of Allah. This was Baba's first direct direction for his religious unity. There were many people in Shirdi who respected Baba. However, he had no companion, comrade or devotee like Shyama or Mhalsapathi among his Muslim followers. The advent of Abdulla imparted a deeper meaning to Muslim faith around Sai Baba's personality.

Abdulla was a loyal, obedient aspirant. He was an ideal sadhaka of Islamic style. No local Muslim knew Baba well in his proper avataric perspective. Bade Baba, Chhote Khan, Abdul Rangari and others came to Shirdi from distant areas in later days of Baba's life. Abdulla was only nineteen-year-old when Baba reached his fifty-fifth year. He lived with Baba and served him for about twenty-eight years, and after Baba's samadhi, he looked after his turbat and collected his sayings and preachings for future generations to benefit.

Abdulla Is Welcomed in the Masjid

In 1890, Shama, Kashiram, Tatya and others were sitting with Baba in the mosque, when Abdulla came. Baba told them that he was his crow and would clean the mosque and the pathways leading to Lendi Baug, Tapovana and will store water for Dwarkamai. Abdulla also undertook the work of lighting the mosque, washing Baba's clothes and earthen pots. Baba undertook the responsibility of looking after Abdulla's spiritual well-being and Islamic training, including reading and study of the sacred Quran. Abdul would also look after Chawdi. Baba told everybody that the young fakir would live with him until his samadhi and look after the turbat after that. He would keep the record of Baba's teachings and guide bhaktas even after Baba leaves his mortal coil. Abdulla became an example or an ideal of modesty and service, learning Muslim type of spiritual discipline under Baba's direct control and supervision, setting an example to the Muslim folk about the mission of an incarnation and Muslim discipleship. Abdulla's example taught Hindus and Muslims on how they can follow their own faith without friction or faction with the followers of other faiths and spiritual disciplines. This was a demonstration of religious coexistence.

Mhalsapathi and Shyama

These two Hindu devotees were also Baba's faithful followers. Mhalsapathi was not an educated man as was Abdulla, but his loyalty and faith was deep. Shyama was a comrade of Baba but he lacked the depth of Abdulla and Mhalsapathi. Mhalsapathi and Abdulla treated Baba as God and adored Baba in their own ways with utmost loyalty. Baba kept Mhalsapathi away from money and greed. He lived in poverty and austere devotion until he left his body and joined his soul to Baba's own soul. These three prepared the background for the coming of Chandorkar and Ganu, who were learned and educated bhaktas with higher intellectual as well as devotional stature.

The Udi and Begging Round

The practice of granting udi as a symbol of grace continued in Shirdi right from 1870, when Baba gradually adjusted to the masjid life. Baba used udi as medicine or Allah's blessings to his devotees. Udi was indicative of the end of life in ashes. It also symbolized the eternal life of the soul, which rises over the mundane limits and shackles. The udi was the bond of protection at the hands of Sai Krishna who was the Lord of Geeta and Bhagwat. It joined the heart of an innocent destitute devotee towards the glory as well as succour from Baba. Baba's begging at the doors of five householders as described in earlier chapters continued during this period. Baba moved in the hot dust bare-footed at noontime and begged for alms. Blessed were the householders who received Baba and gave him food and bread!

15

Enlightening Nana and Ganu, Harbingers of New Transformation

We have delineated with emphasis how the period 1890 to 1918 was the brighter half of Sai life story, wherein he expanded the boundaries of his mission and attracted educated, knowledgeable and loyal men and women to Shirdi fold. Together with men of faith, personalities with erudition, authority, celebrity and penance stepped in Baba's Shirdi. Abdulla was a symbol of Muslim aspirant of Islamic faith and sadhana style who lived in amity with Hindu devotees with full tolerance and understanding. He never deviated from his peculiar religious trends and spiritual diction. He was followed by Nana and Ganu with their profound faith and study of Indian culture with bhakti and dhyana style of Geeta, Bhagwat and Marathi saint literature. This was a step forward in his avataric mission.

The Revolutionary Chapter of 1892

Nana Chandorkar was a religious, pious, merited, moral and learned man. He was Chitnis to the Collector of Ahmednagar. He was specially invited by Baba to the mosque by deputing Appa Kulkarni to Ahmednagar. Nana refused to come, as he had no regard for a fakir in the Shirdi village mosque. Baba repeated his calls and Nana finally accepted to come. He was not sure whether he was a fakir, aulia or saint. But when he stepped in, he was lured by Baba's lustre and infatuated by his atmic attraction. He held Baba's feet and did not want to leave him. Still he asked the reason why Baba called him all of a sudden. Baba explained that there was certainly a reason why he alone was called. Nana was related with Baba for last four births. Baba knew this, while Nana was ignorant of his past births. Nana accepted Baba's invitation to visit the mosque occasionally. He spread Baba's glory in elite and educated circles. He caused the mosque to be renovated and asked Nimonkar to supervise the task. Kondaji, Tukaram and Ganuji (all carpenters) did the work. Baba had great regard for these carpenters as well. Das Ganu also came to Shirdi as a police guard of Nana. His faith in Baba grew later. Originally, he was fond of lavani, tamasha and lewd literature. But he was an inspired poet and had potency as a *kirtankar* (singer of religious songs) and a biographer of saintly persons. Baba changed him into a true devotee through various miracles, astounding experiences and finally nurtured him into a saintly writer himself. Nana and Ganu spread the glory of Baba beyond Shirdi to Bombay, Pune and other rural and urban areas of Maharashtra since 1893 until the end of their own life. The mould and making of Nana and Ganu was gradually developed, transformed and elevated by the grace of Sai Baba.

Nana and Geeta Teachings

Once Nanasaheb Chandorkar was massaging Baba's feet and murmuring some stanza from Bhagwad Geeta. Baba desired to know the stanza. Nana thought Baba was alien to Geeta so he reluctantly recited that stanza, stating that spiritual Masters are pleased by the service and modesty of their true disciples. When they are asked with humility to impart knowledge, they reveal knowledge and pass it on to the disciples. Baba was pleased with Nana's version of the sloka but he pointed out that the term 'dhyana' in the line 'Upadekshanti Te Dhyanam' was out of context. The word 'dhyana' must be replaced by the phrase 'adhyana' (ignorance). Nana told Baba that the term dhyana was accepted by all commentators of Geeta including Shankaracharyaji. Yet Baba did not approve the term. He said that dhyana is self-explanatory or self-established. It does not require explanation. It is discovered when the adhyana is identified and expelled. Nana was astounded with Baba's version. He realized that Baba knew Geeta fully and its interpretation for he was the Lord of Geeta. He was Madhava himself who came down to reinterpret Geeta. When the curtain of falsity is unveiled, the truth is apparently visible. Truth is the same as love or God. Thus, Nana was learning the true meaning of bhakti, dhyana, karma and yoga as contained in Hindu scriptures texts under the shade of Baba's presence. Nana learned the essence of devotion (which was the same as the faith, dedication and surrender) from Sai Baba. Abdulla learnt tolerance and secularism in Baba's presence. Both were symbols of two religions and religious precepts demonstrated in practical terms. They were two faiths running parallel.

The Direction of Aspirant Lifestyle

Abdulla learnt the Quran, Muslim sadhana and lifestyle from Sai Baba, while Chandorkar learnt the philosophy of Bhagwat cult. Baba coached and trained Chandorkar with practical events and experiences, which ultimately led him to the convictions of philosophical precepts of Hinduism. Whenever Nana was disillusioned by weal and woe, power and fortune in life, Baba asked him to dedicate all desires, passions, emotions, sentiments, thoughts, longings and designs at his feet. He asked Nana in the strain of Lord Krishna of Bhagwad Geeta that he should perform his duties dispassionately, without an eye for the fruit or reward. All burdens should be placed on Baba's able shoulders. There should be no ego nurtured in the mind that he was the doer of karma. He should dedicate the doership to his Guru or God. He should remain unattached to body, sense and sensual pleasures. The walls of selfishness and self-centred ego should be demolished. Only then Baba would enter into his soul directly and lead him towards ultimate welfare, as Lord Krishna had led the chariot of his devotee, Arjuna. He asked for Rs 16.50 from Nana. Those sixteen and a half rupees comprised of ten organs, the five senses, ego and half-maya. He explained to Nana that devotion does not mean idol worship, sacrifice, mantra-tantra or japa. It is surrender to Guru and God. He promised Nana that he would lead him to light or the abode of anand through grace. Baba taught Nana the essence of Upanishads (Vedanta) and made him fit to lead an able life of householder devotee. Nana presented in himself a demonstration of love between God and his devotee. The coming of Nana was a landmark in Baba's life as an avatar and manifestation as universal Guru.

Nana and Guru Era

The period of fifteen years, commencing from 1890, was stamped with the mark of Nanasaheb and Das Ganu. The period was of development of these two devotees for propagation of Sai era. It includes several incidents and events in the life of these two great followers of Baba who ushered in the sainthood and avatarhood of Sai Baba. These two luminaries outshadowed other bhaktas like Shyama, Mhalsapathi, Kote and other local families. When the Moon and the Venus rise in the sky, the other smaller stars lose their lustre and separate identity. The other luminaries like Sathe, Dixit, Radhakrishna, Bhishma, Kushabhau and Upasani arrived later between 1905 and 1915 and pervaded the Shirdi sky. Until then, the two great devotees, Nana and Ganu, were shining luminiscently in Shirdi and Sai era. In these days, the influence and fame of Baba as a saint and avatar occupied all quarters of Maharashtra and adjacent areas in a gradual and phased manner. The glory of Sai Baba as Satchitananda Satguru was the real truth and essence of his glory and spiritual mastery. His stature as a universal Guru was self-established. Only proper men of knowledge and sadhana had to arrive between 1905 and 1915 to recognize, discover and appreciate its dazzling lustre and colossal glory of Baba's latent avatarhood.

Das Ganu's Development

We must take into account Ganu's rising in stature in the manner we analysed Nana's development. He came to Shirdi as a police guard of Nana. He had dual loyalty as Shiv bhakta chanting Guru mantra received from his earlier Guru Wamanshastri Islampurkar. He was a Warkari of Pandharpur and a devotee of Vithal as well. Baba inspired faith in him, turned his lyre to the singing of glory of saints, melted his dualism to recognize unity of godheads. He was trained, as Nana was, through several experiences. He finally left the police force and retired into the active life of propagator of the mahima of gods and saints in prose and poetry. He was a kirtankar and his sermons roused and inspired devotion in the hearts of his audience. He spread Baba's mahima everywhere in later years. The alchemy of Baba's grace raised Ganu's low earth to heavenly heights. We will deal with Nana and Ganu more in future chapters.

Baba's Mystery of Form

As understanding about Baba developed, devotees were astounded to see him as Ram, Krishna, Dattatreya, Shiva and Amba. They were puzzled to think of his true divinity as he manifested all godheads within himself. He was sportive in leelas. Majority of followers recognized Baba as Lord Krishna or Guru Dattatreya himself sporting in Dwarka. The flow of devotees rose. People came to repair their destiny and fruits of past karmas. Baba had to ask them for dakshina to teach them the lesson of *tyaga* (sacrifice). The acceptance of dakshina started late in 1903 as a common sacrifice from bhaktas. But even in early days of 1892, Baba asked for dakshina from a few greedy visitors. This was inevitable, as karma accumulated by past ill deeds cannot be repaired without abandonment or sacrifice of attachment and lust for worldly pleasures.

16

Teaching Imparted to Das Ganu and Chandorkar with Divine Experiences

*I*n the last two chapters, we covered Nana Chandorkar and Das Ganu Maharaj, their advent and gradual development on account of company of Sai Baba's Guruhood and the power of grace, which brought about changes in their mental and material make-up and lifestyle. Baba developed a saint poet from Ganu's crudeness and carved a Geeta-style dhyana bhakti aspirant out of Nana. Within fifteen years, Baba transformed the worm into a firefly. This was the alchemy of the miraculous powers of the Shirdi saint.

We have seen that Baba was demonstrating his magical alchemy in changing Nana and Ganu through vision experiences and life events. Baba was protecting Nana, who he said was related to him from past four incarnations. Once, Nana was climbing the Harishchandra Hill to visit the Devi Temple at its top. He was accompanied by his collect orate associates like one Mr Kharawandikar and others. There was no water on the way and Nana was dying of thirst, remembering Baba on the slope of the ascending hill. Baba exclaimed in Dwarkamai, 'O, Nana is panting for water. I must go and provide water to him,' and hit his wooden stick on the ground. On the hill, there appeared a Bhil in front of Nana, who directed him to a stream of water under the rock on which they rested. When a portion of the rock was dislodged, water sprang out in sufficient quantity to quench the thirst of Nana and his companions. When he arrived in the mosque later, Baba reminded him of the incident and the providential help. Nana said that there would be no want when Sai provided grace and succour, even at the testing hour, when all doors of help seem to be closed. This was a direct experience of Baba's unbound help. Nana's faith was gradually nurtured by Baba with practical experiences.

Ganu Drifts to Faith and Patience

Ganu gathered a bit of respect for Baba on account of Nana's experiences, but he had no true devotion or spiritual discipline. Coincidently, a pious spiritual man namely Wamanshastri Islampurkar came into his contact, who initiated Ganu in Shiv mantra and made him move on the path of sadhana. Ganu was a Vithal lover and a Warkari, visiting Pandharpur. He now became a Shiva worshipper as well. At the end of his spiritual career, Wamanshastri asked Ganu to serve Sai Baba for his further progress. Ganu, who visited Shirdi in 1892–93, made a long way progress up to 1895. Baba had decided to transform the police department mentality, nature and psychology of Ganu and make him a servant of saints, a worshipper of Bhagwat style devotional way and a poet–saint and composer. This opportunity became available to Ganu in the Vaikuntha as well as Kailash that was Shirdi, habitated by Sai Baba. Baba inculcated in Ganu's mind the unity of Shiva and Vishnu and the glory of saints who were messengers of God on earth. Baba showed Ganu a direction of celestial light. His sadhana gained potency, velocity and goal. Ganu changed to such an extent that he resigned from the police department and became a kirtankar, and a poet, sang glory of saints and wrote of life stories of living and departed saints. Baba made so many changes in Ganu's life, which gave him multiple experiences, saved him from disasters and made pure gold out of his crude metallic ingredients and inferior constituents of his earlier personality. Baba had to burn the stale stuff out of him to give him a new birth as saint–poet or divine bard singing the glory of Lord.

An Idol of Compassion

Das Ganu's approach to Sai Baba altered in a major way, when Wamanshastri guided him spiritually. Baba convinced Ganu about his colossal spiritual glory. Ganu's heart melted; his doubts and disputing mind subsided. The derisive bent of mind straightened. The practical tone of police career changed into selfless devotion. He exerted to merge his mind into Baba's mahima. He saw Baba as a loving mother, fondling father and compassionate God. He came nearer to Nana in faith and loyalty of sentiment. Ganu sang, 'You are the master. I am your foot-soldier. You are the saviour, I am a destitute.' (*Sai Geetayan*). He declared that he was fed up with the ways of material world. He now yearned for merger in Baba alone. This depth made him choke with emotion and his eyes flooded with water. The eight pious sentiments arose in his mind. He saw Baba as Vithal standing on the brick of faith. He desired that this Pandurang, Lord of Pandhari, should manifest in his heart. He wrote such beautiful *abhangas* (short poems) like 'Shirdi is my Pandhari and Sai Baba is my Vithal', which are drenched in deep love and devotional urge, and are immortal in Sai literature.

The Ganges Flows from Baba's Feet

Being a visitor of Pandharpur, Ganu had latent love and deep urge for Vithal's vision. The recitation of Shiva mantra was drifting him from bhakti to dhyana. Once on a Shivaratri, Ganu sought Baba's permission to bathe in the Godavari, which was four miles away. Baba knew that Ganu's duality in separating Shiva from Vishnu was damaging his spiritual progress and must be erased and replaced by Advaita knowledge. Baba refused him permission and said that Ganga was at his feet. And lo! The streams of the Ganges and the Yamuna sprouted from Baba's feet in big fountains. The unity of Shiva and Vishnu resided in Baba's divinity. There was no space for doubt. Baba was dhyana Shiva and bhakti Mukunda at once in an indivisible form. The doubts and duality melted at once.

Nana Preached Moksha in Sansaric Life—Baba's Unique Way

Baba was coaching and preparing Nana and Ganu simultaneously to be a part of his avatarhood work. He exposed them to the realities of life while they were tossed through light and shade, weal and woe, victory and defeat in the waves of oceanic life. Once Nana urged Baba to free his soul from the ups and downs of life and merge it into bliss. Baba told him that the moksha is to be achieved by detached attitude towards life. One cannot run away from life and wed himself to emancipation. The liberation is the fruit of sadhana in living life itself. The relatives, friends, success, failure in life are illusory. Attachments are caused by desire. The sansar is not limited to house, wife and fortune. Every act, every longing creates sansar. Baba told Nana that mind itself is the seed of sansar and new birth. The sansar will not end until the mind evaporates and turns into no-mind. Baba said, 'Nana, you have to remain in sansar. The mind, intellect and ego should be immersed in God's love. When body consciousness ends, God enters in life. Merge your consciousness in me. I will lead you out of the ocean of sansar. The sansar or birth is an end-product of karma or prarabdha. We shall have to be quiet, unattached, in the waves of prarabdha without involving our ego or doership in acts. The bond of karma will not end until I and mine ends. The doer is God alone. The chain of binding karma (emanating from ego) must be broken. Meditate on Guru. Do not indulge in sense pleasures. Dedicate karmas and their fruit to God. Do your duty selflessly without any ego involvement. This will establish God as your life charioteer who will lead your life cart to the town of liberation. You have to sit in the back seat in dedication and surrender.'

'Sing the Glory of Saints with Love, O Ganu'

Das Ganu also was being trained by Baba with innumerable experiences, i.e. turning the earth of his life stuff into gold. Ganu's individuality was rising in manifold aspects and phases. He met a number of hardships and debacles in government service and was fed up with the servitude. Baba saved him several times and Ganu also longed for promotion but preferred emancipation from the bonds of gold. Once there was a major robbery by the side of his police station and he was highly censured and degraded; but soon the robbers were caught by sheer coincidence and luck. As a result, Ganu got promoted. He was deputed to detect hiding places of formidable dacoit named Kana Bhil. He posed as a Ramdasi bhakta sevak in a Hanuman Temple in hilly regions of Nagar District. Kana doubted the Ramdasi who was wearing police footwear but he took pity on Ganu who wept for his life. Kana Bhil let him go away. Soon Ganu got rid of the assignment by pretending indisposition due to heart trouble. He secretly avowed to leave the job by releasing 'Tilanjali' water, as offering in token of the vow. Still he hid from Baba's view. Baba saw everything through and through and made him resign from police force, assuring him protection and provision of initial sustenance. Baba told him, 'Ganu, you are not born to polish the boots of your superiors. There are bosses above your bosses. You must serve the ultimate supreme boss of the universe (Allah). You invite saints for meals (*bhojan*), and serve them food in the form of writing their biographies and poems depicting their glory to public at large (i.e. to the devotional world of the contemporary days).' Ganu resigned from the police department in 1903 and composed *Santa Katha Mruta, Arvachin Bhakta Leelamrut* and *Bhakta Saramrut*. He also composed *Sai Stavana Manjiri*, commented on the Upanishads and wrote sweet songs on Baba's love such as 'Shirdi Maze Pandharapura', 'Sai Raham Nazara Karna', etc. He started delivering sermons on spiritualism. The life stories of dead and living saints and sadhus were the subjects of his kirtans. He inspired love for saints, introduced Sai Baba as a saint and an avatar before the devotional men and women in urban and rural Maharashtra. The scintillating stories attracted large sectors of devotees to Shirdi. He wore no shirt or headcloth. He sang with an ektari (simple lyre) in his hand. He did not collect money. He distributed his earning to the poor after retaining a fraction for his subsistence and journey expenses. He helped to rebuild samadhis and repair temples in Maharashtra. This was the first discovery of Baba's true self as the universal Guru principle.

The Guru Principle

The avataric mission of Baba assumed shape and form through Nana and Ganu. To them, Baba was not a mere saint or sadhu. People were fascinated by his avatarhood, which touched the meridian and brought all religions, castes and creed under singular umbrella of Allah Malik. He was the *banda* (servant) of his Sarkar (Dattatreya or Fakir Guru). The Guru or God was supreme principle. Baba was a messenger or apostle of universal or cosmic God. He had come to exhibit the power and colossal glory of the Supreme power or Supreme principle pervading all. Baba explained to Nana that His fakir God ruled the entire universe. Nobody can fathom His power, depth or potency. He was beyond time, space, destiny. This power was occult and unknown to words or logic, but it was only accessible to love, faith, surrender and dedication. We have to ask for the immeasurable wealth of liberation from cosmic Guru (not for mundane gifts and boons of vanishing nature).

Comrade at Testing Hour

Baba proved and convinced Nana that faith and surrender mixed with untainted love brought down God's grace to man. During 1902–3, when Nana was posted as Tehsildar at Jamner, Nana's daughter was suffering delivery pangs and the position of the child was such at the time of delivery that she was facing imminent death. Nana prayed to Baba ardently. When Baba came to know the plight of Maina (Nana's daughter), he suddenly called for Bapugir from Khandesh who was returning to his home village. He gave Adkar's arti, namely '*Arti Sai Baba*', and the sacred udi to Bapugir and ordered him to leave for Jalgaon. Bapugir only had Rs 2 for the ticket, but Baba, with his occult powers, created a four-wheeler baggi, horses and a baggi driver to take Bapugir to Nana's place. Soon as Bapugir reached his destination, the driver, the baggi and the horses disappeared into thin air. He gave the udi and the arti to Nana, which helped give instant relief to his ailing daughter. It was a miraculous recovery. Maina delivered a male child and Nana got a grandson. In gratitude, Nana prayed for Baba's compassion and praised his greatness. Baba was an avatar of Datta in Kali Yuga, a conditioned form of Brahma. Baba can be equated to the Satchitananda principle behind the cosmos. This greatness of Baba as Guru was later acknowledged fully when more ardent, progressed devotees like Sathe, Bhishma, Kushabhau, Upasani and others came to Shirdi to celebrate Guru Purnima, fully appreciating Baba's avataric mystery as Guru in cosmic form. This was the true nature and glory of the sainthood and avatarhood of Shirdi Sai Baba. This was the beginning of teaching Shirdi devotees and followers about the true nature of God and *moksha* (salvation) sadhana.

Knowledge of Brahma

Baba was training great bhaktas and opening the eyes of ignorant men as well as those who approached him with wrong purpose and wrong concepts. A rich sethji thought that Brahma could be realized by visiting Sai Baba. He approached Baba and expressed his desire to Baba through Shyama. He did not know that realization of Brahma presupposed penance and sacrifice of greed and six *vikaras* (sins). Baba asked for five rupees from various individuals in Shirdi, while the seth waited in the mosque for darshan of Brahma with Rs 250 in his pocket. He did not understand why Baba wanted Rs 5 from others. When the sethji became impatient to see Brahma, Baba lashed out and reprimanded him that a greedy and selfish man of his type would never see even a glimpse of Brahma. To have the vision of God or Brahma, a man has to sacrifice his mind, intellect, body and ego and become fully surrendered to Guru or God. The individual must be pious, and without lure or lust for material pleasures or gains to reach Brahma. Everybody must note that the purity of body, mind, intellect and ego is necessary for sadhana leading to liberation. The Guru Geeta has explained that external things like donating, seeing holy places, fastings, japa and austerities do not enjoin oneself to moksha. One has to concentrate and meditate on the form of Guru incessantly, so that the Guru has the compassion to lift his soul and awareness beyond all material bonds and join his consciousness to divine consciousness.

17

Tenets of Faith and Surrender

*B*aba's sainthood now assumed enormous proportions embracing entire skyline of religions, castes and sects.

In the later years, this avatarhood of Baba became still wider and expansive as cosmic Guru (the Satchitananda form), the master of innumerable galaxies of the cosmos. Baba posed himself during earlier years as an apostle of cosmic Guru and told that the grace of this Guru descends through surrender and dedication, which is the secret of bhakti. Guru was supreme, omnipotent and the ultimate master.

O Madhav, This Sarkar Is Marvellous

The Sarkar (cosmic Guru) was a marvel. The governing power of Baba's Sarkar expects nothing but *shraddha* (faith) and *saburi* (dedication, preparedness to tolerate discomforts for ultimate welfare). Baba posed himself as an executive of the limitless cosmic power of his Sarkar until the advanced aspirants like Bhishma, Kushabhau, Upasani Maharaj appeared on the Shirdi stage. He said that there was no power higher than Guru Datta. He told Chandorkar that he would not grace those who avoid darshan of Lord Dattatreya. He clarified that Guru operated through saints who were executives of Lord. He confessed that he loved dedicated devotees, though he was inscrutable even to Vedantas and religious texts. He told Madhavrao that the Sarkar was a mystery. Guru supported entire universe, although he was supportless Brahma. He himself was a messenger of the Guru. The nature of Guru was bliss or ananda. He is sovereign with the sceptre of love. He sported as Mukunda in the heart of deep sentiment. He did not desire flowers, water or fruit. He wants surrender of self. Sarkar is born in the selfless, lovelorn heart and is reared in cradle of pure sentiments.

Faith and Surrender

Guru wants only two coins of faith and surrender as dakshina for himself. Faith is deeper than emotion. It is the awareness of his majestic presence all the time. Mixture of thought and sentiment is not faith. It is awareness based on discrimination and conscious attention, which joins us to the Guru. Saburi is not courage or manliness. It is perseverance that observes the waves of prarabdha without involvement or indulgence. It is detached factual approach to the destiny. It gives durability, tenacity, inspiration and endurance to bhakta with true faith. It is not worldly affair. It is an attitude towards Hara. On the love front, he is Hari; on the knowledge front, he is Hara (Shiva). He obviates body sense and immerses a devotee in the well of no-mind and the aspirant becomes one with the bliss or ecstatic state of universal merger. This is the working style of Guru. This is the true essence of Baba's shraddha and saburi.

Guru Controls Elements

Once Shirdi was flooded by incessant rains, thunderstorm, lightning and holocaust of hurricane. It was a doomsday. Bhaktas prayed to Baba. Baba, out of compassion, gave a cry to the universal master to control Indra, Varuna and Vayu, the elements ravaging the atmosphere. The call to Guru calmed down the wrath of the elements and the storm subsided. The village revived with glee. Shirdi was saved from the deluge. Abdulla treated Baba as his Guru and noted down all the utterances and words of Baba, which later guided those who came to seek help. Baba gave him siddhi of occult guidance through the pages of his written book.

Raobahadur H.V. Sathe was the Deputy Collector and Settlement officer of Ahmednagar. He treated Baba as his Guru since he met Baba in 1904. He got married late and had a male child with Baba's grace. He served Baba by erecting a thatch on Chawdi and building Sathe Wada for his own stay and for devotees' sojourn in Shirdi. Such facilities were nil or scarce then. Megha, a Gujarati Brahmin purohit, served Sathe. He was directed by Sathe to worship Baba. Megha thought Sai Baba was a Muslim, but soon he realized that Baba was Shiva himself, whom he had adored for years with deep faith. Megha's greatness in disciplehood was recognized by Baba himself who wept on his demise in 1912 and bore the expenses of his funeral rites.

Collective Worship (Sagunopasana)

Collective or congregational worship of Guru started in Shirdi as early as 1905–6, when Sathe sent Megha to Shirdi. It grew and emblazoned the horizon of Shirdi and surroundings in the later twelve years, which was a golden period in avataric and Guruhood phase of life of Baba. This particular period under review was the beginning of the most illuminated phase of Baba's life and mission as an avatar of cosmic Guru. This last phase was a concrete stage of development of Baba's glory or the unfoldment of his mission for which he came back to life in 1886 and assumed the responsibility of a wider movement of uplifting universal humanity. The stature of Guru (cosmic principle) was the reality of Baba's personality and sainthood. No other power than Lord Dattatreya (Shripad Shri Vallabha) can be compared or identified with Shirdi Sai Baba in the later phase of his life, when he assumed his full glory and capacity as Satchitananda Swaroopa. Sai Baba was really the Satchitananda; Guru principle fully controlling the flora and fauna, mankind and the cosmos. Baba was limitless Brahma as well as universal paramatma. This reality of his glory could not be discovered or assessed in the earlier years of Baba's life. Time has to prepare itself first to probe the depth of the supreme divinity of a supreme Master.

18

Baba's Sainthood Rises to Guruhood

We have here introduced our readers to lesser known and obscure portion of the saints' physical existence on this planet which required special emphasis, search and exposition to bring home the correct, just and pragmatic visualization of the undiscovered spells. The magnetic pull of Baba was to bring Abdulla, Chandorkar and Ganu within the aura of love, i.e. Shirdi. This was his mission after coming back from Allah's home in 1886 and undertaking new and revived colossal task. Baba had to expand the compromising religion taught by Guru Nanak and Kabir. He was on the threshold of new and old worlds to proclaim his new undertaking of uniting God concepts, spiritual sects and launch humanity on the platform of equality and self-welfare.

Nine-fold Bhakti and Dhyana, Bhakti, Karma, Yoga

The Indian spiritualism is constituted by karmic Vedic lore, Vedantic thought enunciated by Upanishads, the self-discipline of Shiva yoga, and the devotional overflow of Bhagwat philosophy. However, the basic and rudimental undercurrent of Indian culture is the confluence of dhyana bhakti professed by Lord Krishna in Geeta and lovelorn devotion of Bhagwat, which are assimilated in the vital breath of India. It is for this reason that every saint or incarnation has to harmonize dhyana and bhakti cult for the edification of their followers, whenever they start an epoch-making mission or religious agitation. The avataric background of Baba's mission had an altogether different context. He was neither an author nor sermonizing orator. He had created some symbolic ideals around him by his multifaceted teachings and his omnipotent willing power. The segment of time prior to 1905 also bears the landmarks of these ideals. We have to discuss here some conceptions and instances in this direction. Baba touched certain individuals around him and changed their character in such a way that they would exemplify themselves as ideals of vandana, archana, sakhya, dasya, shravan (listening) and atma nivedan (communication) types of bhakti.

Mhalsapathi and Megha (Their Worship and Adoration Type of Devotion)

Baba, through these two devotees, could develop ideals of archana, vandana and pujan bhakti, making optimum use of their loyalty, detachment and faith. Mhalsapathi lived in detachment, away from lust for money and passed his days in dire poverty and destitution. He loved Baba with loyalty and performed his vandana, archana bhakti after he had worshipped all village deities. Baba made his devotion fruitful and raised him to Shiva loka by his grace. Another ideal devotee was Megha. His intensely passioned and sentimental devotion was accepted and rewarded by Baba only after the discrimination in his mind about religion and caste was wiped off. Baba refined his devotion with knowledge. He wept when Megha died and lamented like an ignorant being to honour his loyalty and to teach the idealism to other devotees of this type. Baba bore the expenses of his funeral and uplifted Megha to Kailash loka. There were other Hindus and Muslims who prostrated and surrendered before the Eternal principle that was Baba. These were mostly common people like Baija, Ganpatrao, Tatya, Kashiram. Baba treated them as his children and kith and kin, and showed grace on them. For these people pujan, archana, karmakanda (rituals), sadhana, shravan, kirtan, dhyana yoga, atma nivedan, reciting religious books, etc. was not a prerequisite. They were eligible to get the vibrations of grace as Baba's rustic playmates. Baba told them that he was their father and they were eligible to pray and demand whatever they wanted from him. The comrade devotion of Shyama and servant role of Abdulla was unparalleled in the history of devotion as they were unique models of this type of relationship with a godman. Radhakrishna Aai also did service to Baba and his devotees and was an ideal of dasya bhakti in Shirdi. She disciplined the services to the incoming devotees and streamlined the upasana with the necessary paraphernalia and equipments necessary for an institution of faith and devotion growing around the divinity of Sai Baba. She was an ideal *sevika* (servant) with practical insight. She cleaned the Shirdi lanes, masjid precincts and helped the sojourning visitors. She gained the divine wealth through the service of accumulating valuable accessories of a sansthan like chhatra (umbrella), chamar, rath and material required for congregational worship, which further grew the upasana into an institution of sansthan.

Shyama's Comrade Bhakti and Nana, Ganu, Dengle's Self-Communicating Dhyana Bhakti

Shyama's approach towards and relationship with Baba was rather prosaic and practical. He helped incoming devotees who had desires to get fulfilled through a saint's grace and accomplish selfish purposes along with spiritual lining. Baba realized Shyama's limits but loved him still as he said that Shyama was related to him since past seventy-two generations. The functioning of Shyama as Baba's comrade was materialistic, yet it was conditioned by Baba's divine celestial love and affection for the imperfect and immature man that was Shyama. The love of Shyama, however, could not rise to higher level. It was therefore that Shyama remained untouched by Sai Baba's glory and could not even appreciate the mahima even after his long-standing association with Sai Baba ended. He wept, remembering Baba after his departure. This was Shyama's greatest misfortune. He was steeped in darkness of ignorance under the divine light of Sai Baba. The devotion of Dengle, Ganu and Nana was deep and intense. Their faith was untainted and unequalled. They sought Baba's proximity by constant meditation, contemplation and recollection of his words and deeds, for they were genuine dhyani bhaktas. It was a perpetual Guru remembrance, atma nivedan and a balanced meditation. Not only did they appreciate Baba, his life, his teachings and his mission, they also helped to spread it in all directions by being the wheels in the divine and missionary machinery of Baba's avataric work and purpose. The confluence of knowledge, devotion, yoga and karma was exhibited within the lifespan of the three devotees of high order. Ganu used kirtans, sermons and narrations of saint's biographies to spread Baba's mahima. Chandorkar and Dengle used their personal influence and contacts to spread the recognition of Sai Baba's glory in the official circles as well as the areas of their reach in private and public life. Das Ganu had his lion's share as he was an avowed kirtankar of Maharashtra. However, his dramatic and literary artistry could not reach the depth of the simple and innocent but steadfast, deep and entrenched affection of Megha, Abdulla, Dengle and Chandorkar. This was an observation recorded by learned Sai biographers. I feel that Ganu's devotion was divided among a large number of sadhus, saints and godheads and it was scattered in many directions. He could not focus fully on Sai Baba alone, nor could understand his godhood in its real depth as also its vast expanse.

Dhyana, Bhakti, Karma, Yoga

The teachings of Sai Baba during 1886 to 1905 did not include Vedas and Vedic karmakanda. He did not preach even the rigours of yoga sadhana (Patanjali or Kuṇḍalini). When the Guru shines with full lustre, he does not take recourse to rituals or karmic practices prevalent among mechanical and professional priests and middlemen who preach themselves as agents of religion. Guru is the giver of fruits of all karmas. He is the idol of Satchitananda, which is the final destination of all sadhanas and practices. The universal Guru had incarnated as Sai Baba, who had immense power of all spiritual grace which he showered in abundance on all true, genuine, loyal devotees. He required uninterrupted attention, faith, dedication, love and wholehearted surrender at his feet. He denounced rites, rituals, separatism, mantra-tantra practices, fasting and austerities. He had ample wealth of his Sarkar to impart. His Guru principle after command of Allah now emblazoned the entire skyline. The apprehension of his cosmic potency slowly unfolded after 1905 up to his mahasamadhi and in greater proportions thereafter. This was the most shining golden period of Baba's life which we have to first understand, assess and then to spotlight for the sake of ardent readers who understand Gurushakti. When Gurushakti works, all paths come together and give integrated results.

Dawn of Age of Avataric Mission and Approach

The *sankalpa* (pledge) of the Almighty to get the epoch-making mission of unity of entire humanity and religions being carried out through Sai Baba's incarnation brought Ganu, Chandorkar, Abdulla nearer to him. The eternal (*sanatan*) religion, which is the core of all religions, and brings the human race to the point of perfection, was enunciated by Baba at this stage in his life. The unity of godheads and the equality of man and the dedication and surrender that attracts grace and compassion from the Divine, constituted the new religion of love of Sai Baba. In 1905, Radhakrishna's advent set the chariot of the new dharma into dynamic motion. The Guru principle which prevails beyond time, distance and limitations manifested through Baba's fragile frame since 1909 when Guru puja started in Shirdi. This period attracted stupendous congregation of dhyanis, yogis and pious bhaktas to Shirdi. Their number and strength grew every day upto the mahasamadhi of Sai Baba. It multiplied in enormous proportions after 1918, when Baba assumed cosmic powers and individuality of universal latitude.

Fix Idol of Guru in Heart

Baba used to tell such devotees as Kelkar, Sathe, Dixit, Shyama, Nana, Ganu etc. that they must pay attention to the intense and selfless devotion of Megha, Mhalsapathi and Abdulla. The devotees were not educated or elite but they had innocence, dedication, loyalty and intensity of love for their Guru and God. Baba appreciated such devotion, not the superficial one. The shallow terms of poetry or literature cannot move him. Words must spring from the depth of one's heart and force of sentiment. The ignorant trio may not be learned or well versed in shastras or religious lore, but their yearnings are centred round the form and image of Guru. The educated devotees must follow their faith and love, and imitate this illiterate trio for their benefit. Allah would definitely have grace on such aspirants. Ganu told Baba, 'Baba, it is for you to give us these higher sentiments and stabilize us therein. You are our charioteer, Lord Krishna. We surrender to you for all help.' Baba clarified that surrender and dedication lead a devotee to the godward path through Guru. The lesson of intense love and *seva* (service) karma sprouting from the fountain of love was being taught to Kelkar, Sathe, Ganu, Nana by Abdulla, Megha and Mhalsapathi. Selfless love in one's heart transforms karmas into seva. The actions are yajnas and likewise whole mayic sansara in itself changed into the shape of liberation. The uneducated devotees were virtually the models of such teachings.

Radhakrishna Aai's Love, Devotion and Service

The love and service of madhura bhakti, as embodied in Radhakrishna Aai, reached Shirdi around 1905–06. She was a widow from Pandharpur. She was a beautiful lady and lover of Bal Krishna. She flung herself in devotion and religious pursuits after her husband's demise. Nana Chandorkar, posted at Pandharpur as Tehsildar, appreciated her devotion for the Lord and succeeded in persuading her to Shirdi in the abode of Sai Krishna, the living God. She dedicated her heart and soul to Sai devotion as well as to daily external seva such as cleaning the masjid precincts, sweeping roads and lanes on which Sai Krishna stepped. She looked after the incoming visitors. The congregational upasana like worship, arti, rath and procession started in Shirdi in her presence and supervision. She collected all the equipments and material necessary for such worship and helped Shirdi develop into a centre of worship or institution of adoration. Her love, dedication and sacrifice were exemplary. She attracted, collected and activated the devotees worldwide to make Shirdi an abode of pilgrimage at the initial stages. She gained many siddhis as she was practicing yoga, meditation and higher upasana privately to enrich her spiritual make up. On the other hand, she looked after the sansar of the Sai devotees. Palanquin, chariot procession, chhatra, chamaras and bhaldar, chopdars formed a part of congregational worship at Shirdi, which centred round Baba's divinity. This was a result of the seva and bhakti inspired and brought into practice by Radhakrishna Aai, the current of genuine bhakti. She used to subsist herself on pieces of bread sent by Baba from his bhiksha. Her life of seva came to an end a year prior to Baba's mahasamadhi. The year 1906 to 1918, saw a great change in Shirdi surroundings. The place was full of grandeur and abundance. Bhaktas of low and high order thronged around the Dwarkamai to have darshan and get blessings of Baba. Radhakrishna equalled Abdulla, Megha, Mhalsapathi in devotion and seva but excelled in dhyana, karma, bhakti and yoga which were higher levels of spiritual life.

Readers should note this comparison and contrast with deeper concentration and broad-based understanding to imbibe real values of spiritual life as against external vanity.

Universal Guruhood Envelops Devotees from All Quarters

The dawn of avataric light in Sai Baba's life was visible in 1905, when Ganu and Nana arrived and spread the message of Baba's mission and lustre of sainthood. Kelkar, Sathe, Megha and Radhakrishna ushered in the new era of congregational Guru devotion. The higher spiritual Guru Purnima of the edification, uplift and salvation spread in thousand directions. The identity of Baba's cosmic Guru avatar was felt predominantly which brought about a historical change befitting Indian mysticism and spiritual culture. Guru worshippers of the stature of Sathe, Dixit, Jog, Dhumal, Kelkar, Nulkar, Tarkhad, Bhishma, Kushabhau and Upasani settled around Baba to strengthen the aura of Nana and Ganu. Dabholkar, Bhishma, Ganu, Kushabhau and Upasani were the torch-bearers who illumined the forgotten corners and potencies of Baba's sainthood and avatarhood. This was the congregation of the lovers of God and Guru. However, Baba was seventy-five years old by this time. A great avatar had to live and act for seventy-five years before the ignorant world realized his glory!

Between 1905 and 1909, the place of Baba in the galaxy of Indian saints appeared unique and unparalleled. He was paradoxical but enticing godman; he was away from mob and renounced but was capable of uplifting people above the sansara; he was humanitarian but equal visioned. He was Satchitananda, absolute Brahma. He was an avatar above all mundane levels and parameters. His glory could cross the borders of distance and time, touching, viewing all directions. He once saved a blacksmith's little daughter, who had fallen in a burning furnace, by inserting his hand in the flames of the dhuni in Dwarkamai. His hands got burnt but the child was saved. He knew all about past, present and future. His sankalpa was respected and materialized by maya herself. He acted as an ordinary man although his personality had cosmic dimensions. He mitigated the sufferings of his devotees using his divine powers. He graced virtuous men with love and compassion. He repulsed wicked people but strengthened the faith of the good and pious. Even selfishly motivated people were rewarded by his *karuna* (piety), shraddha and saburi. Their crookedness got moistened into virtue. He made people realize that God dwells not in masjid or mandir but in the hearts of those bhaktas who were loving towards others. He preached that God dwelt in the lovelorn bosom of a devotee, in the discrimination of dhyani, in the balance of karma and in the service of humanity. His saintly avatarhood was really the power of cosmic Guru. His prowess and lustre was his unique Guruhood which enveloped the entire spell of time beyond 1909.

Lord's Dattatreya—The Real Essence of Baba's Inner Self

Sai Baba is the wish-fulfilling tree of liberation, ocean of knowledge, reservoir of love and the Kamdhenu of his devotees' wishes. Although nava-idhis, siddhis and powers were at his feet, his bhaktas never knew about this till his seventy-fifth year. This was understood when Sathe, Dixit, Bhishma, Kushabhau and Upasani came to the scene of Guru worship. Madhav Adkar who wrote the Guru arti, namely *Arti Sai Baba*, much earlier was the harbinger of Baba's advent as Guru. Baba's deposition before one-man Court Commission deputed by Dhule Court to Shirdi was exemplary and reminiscent of his genuine core of Guru identity. Let us discuss these aspects in foregoing paragraphs for Guru form was his real manifestation.

Guru Gaurav (Glory of Guru) in Sai Literature

Madhav Adkar's arti was an old arti, pioneering portrayal of Baba as Lord Dattatreya (Guru avatar). This was included in daily Sagunopasana later by Bhishma. Its potency and effective power was recognized by Baba himself, when he asked Bapugir in 1902–03 to take the arti with holy ashes. Baba's glory as Satchitananda has been eulogized in this arti. Baba as the external cosmic Guru comes with all his powers to save his devotees caught in a plight and rescues them from calamities. The arti is an exercise of spiritual sadhana, which can be experienced. The singer dedicates his soul to Baba with *chitta* (heart), mind, ego, intellect all combined. This surrender attracts grace divine. The arti states that Sai Baba is the modern Guru incarnation in Kali age. This avatar comes down as conditioned Brahma, Lord Datta Guru. It is not necessary to comment on the calamity-averting strength of this arti. Bhishma's poems and Upasani's stanzas in Sanskrit describe Sai as Lord Datta. These are part of daily Sagunopasana at Shirdi and are well known to the devotees of Sai Baba.

'I Am Master of This World; I Am the Munificent Donor'

Baba had given his deposition before Dhule Court Commission in 1906, which explains the true nature of Sai avatar confessed by Baba himself in his statement. A thief, who was arrested and produced before the judge, told the court that the valuables possessed by him were not stolen. Sai Baba of Shirdi had given them to him. The court sent summons to Sai Baba who threw the order in the dhuni. Next, a warrant for his arrest was issued. Chandorkar and others submitted a *darkhast* (application) to the Dhule court that Sai Baba was their revered Guru and a Commissioner should be deputed for the enquiry. Accordingly, a one-man Commission of Shri Nana Joshi arrived in Shirdi, who examined Sai Baba in the Dwarkamai. The replies given by Baba to the Commission were not only astounding and indicative of his timeless divinity but also manifestation of his powers and glory. Baba told Nana Joshi that he was timeless and spaceless. He was beyond all limitations. His caste was God and his sect, Kabir. He was a disciple of Venkusha. His age was innumerable units of time. He gave all things to people according to his free will. No incident, no give-and-take can happen without his consent. This manifested his immeasurable godly power and timeless existence. He was God and Guru and had come for the work divine. He was Rama and Krishna. He was Shiva and Vishnu. He was Sarkar (Guru Dattatreya). He was Shripad Shri Vallabha incarnation who had come to uplift the world.

Symbol of Gurupaduka (Confluence of Cults)

Baba was related to Kabir, Sufi, Nath and Datta cults wherein the relationship between Guru–disciple is the pivotal key to spiritual success. Baba had shown his utmost respect to Roshan Shah's tomb below the neem tree and Venkusha's teachings. This has been amply illustrated. These sadhanas give vital importance to love and obedience to Guru and the grace or *kripa* flowing from him to the disciple which takes the latter to higher levels. Their relationship is a canal or corridor to the flow of divine grace and Guru is the switchboard that controls and operates the passage. There is nothing greater or nobler than the compassion of Guru and faith and loyalty of a disciple. There are no bonds so relieving, alleviating, liberating, uplifting and emancipating that can at the same time be selfless, undemanding, pure and auspicious. The relation which leads human kinship to ultimate realization cannot be assessed as it is divine, unequalled and unparalleled. Mere words cannot describe the glory of Guru. The Guru is more loving than a mother, cooler than moonbeams. Guru comes with the love and compassion of parents and power and majesty of the Lord. The nature and core of Guruhood cannot be assessed by philosophy (shastras). Guru comes down to the need of his surrendered, dedicated children on earth. He incarnates for the salvation of humanity through the greatest and the best saints, sadhus, Siddhas and Masters in a century and edifies, guides and uplifts the human race. He leads humanity from darkness to light, from ignorance to knowledge, from death to immortality. Such is his love and compassion. He is Yogeshwar among yogis, he is Dhyaneshwar among dhyanis and he is Parmeshwar (God) among devotees. Sai Baba, Swami Samarth, Shripad Shri Vallabha and other great Masters were manifestations

Kundaliniguru
Shri Bamanrao Gunbani
Maharaj

Tajuddinbaba

Nathpanthiguru
Dr. Bitthalrao Gh

Guru Parampara of Author

of the trinity of Lord Dattatreya (the eternal Guru) on the stage of universal drama. This is the mystery, prowess and purpose of Guru incarnation. Guru is not an individual, idol or personification of power. He is uplifting and liberating amrita principle. The appreciation of Sai Baba as Guru started from 1905 to 1909. The upasana of Sai Baba as Guru principle started in 1909. The Guru cult of Baba was recognized and followed since 1910 upto his samadhi in 1918. Then Baba did not remain an obscure fakir or donator of blessings of Allah. The command of Allah to Baba to act as an incarnation of the age ordained in 1886 became fruitful in 1909–10. Baba first repudiated all projections of bhaktas, treating him as a Guru. He directed the aspirants towards a pole in the Dwarkamai, opposite the dhuni, where a picture of Shripad Vallabha hung and told them that the Guru principle is dwelling in the entire universe from Brahma to the pole. He really appreciated the puja of symbolic feet of Dattatreya as Guru manifestation rather than worshipping a living saint as Guru. But gradually he accepted Guru puja for he was the true Guru principle himself. Devotees like Bhishma, Kushabhau, Upasani, Ganu, Nana, Dixit, Sathe, Dhumal, Dabholkar and such men of knowledge came to Shirdi by that time. They were all fully aware that Baba was the eternal Guru. His power is inherent in occult symbols or signs such as bana lingas, padukas or Guru manifestations. He is at once saguna beyond the padukas and at the same time nirguna dormant in padukas. The sadhakas have to search him on such sensitive borders of known and unknown, manifested and unmanifested, wherefrom he can appear at any time at the behest of ardent devotees, for he is always a roving, moving and dynamic shakti treading and traversing the entire universe, in search of deserving followers, worthy to be graced.

Dattavadhoot Moves On

The uplifting power of Lord Dattatreya was working through the fakir in Sai Baba from the very beginning but its acknowledgement came only in 1905–09. Lord Dattatreya remains dormant and unintelligible to ignorant minds and manifests before only those who ardently and frantically search and apprehend his presence.

Baba's command, 'You look to me and I shall look to you,' is the ordaining of *Shri Guru Geeta*. Devotees came to understand that this is exactly the version of *Guru Geeta* phrase 'Dhyanamoolam Gurormurti'. Dedication and surrender to Guru is the essence of Guru upasana. Baba was an exemplary disciple, who lived near the samadhi of his Guru. He nurtured a garden of marigold and roses near it. He chose the dust pit behind his Guru's turbat for his own samadhi. We have explained how Baba made Buti erect a platform for Krishna idol in the mandir, which became his last repose after the samadhi. Baba's biography in itself is a Guru Charitra. His life is Guru Katha. Baba once revealed how his Guru tied him upside down in a well and stabilized his mind, i.e. turned his mana into unmana state. Gazing at the face and eyes of the Guru was his sadhana. He lit his flame of heart against the flame of Guru and himself became Satchitananda! He told that Rama and Krishna have now come as Sai Baba. He asked everybody to hold him fast by hand of shraddha and saburi. He would carry his bhaktas beyond the ocean of maya. His mantra was that he was ours and we were his own. He had donned the attire of a fakir to shower compassion and love. He asked devotees to call him Satchitananda Satguru, so that he would appear with the true majesty of Guru. Dhyana, bhakti, karma and yoga would carry a sadhaka to certain stage but beyond that, automatic gears of Guru kripa operate. It is therefore desirable to hold Baba's hand at the outset only. He had the wealth of his Guru in abundance in his farm. But no deserving man came to harvest the crop, which he was only too eager to dole out. He fulfilled the small demands of devotees so that they would ultimately ask for what Baba wanted to give them of his own choice. He wanted the devotees to surrender their body, mind, intellect and ego at his feet and make selfless demands of the timeless, ageless fortune (the moksha) from his Guru. He himself begged at the doors of his devotees so that they desire to accept the Guru's unending wealth of liberation. He accepted this dakshina, so that he could lift us above the tossings of the ocean of sansara. God begs so that devotees desire liberation.

20

Baba's Association with Villagers in Earlier Days

The events in Sai Baba's life, as reflected in *Sai Satcharitra* by Hemadpant and other books, lack a logical and chronological order. In addition, the passing mention or reference to certain names does not fit properly in a historical sequence. The persons manifest for a moment and then disappear in years earlier to 1905. Many renowned devotees have, however, found place in the biography during 1905–18. The period prior to this records some unforgettable personalities (although they were uneducated and belonged to common village society) like Tatya, Baija, Mhalsapathi, Sathe, Dixit, Buti, Bhishma who have also laid a deep impression on the life of Baba. However, we know very little about aspirant devotees like Bhishma, Kushabhau, Upasani, Kelkar, Sathe, etc. only because Hemadpant has not dealt with them at length. Let us try to touch and bring to light some of the small and big men of this type who were deeper in spiritual sadhana than those who were nearer to the author of *Sai Satcharitra*.

People Who Touched Sai's Life

It is high time that we recapitulate the names and events of significance connected with Sai Baba. We have already discussed some persons in this book and would like to add some more, whether small or big, ignorant or advanced in spiritual life. No one may be totally forgotten or ignored only because the authoritative and popular biography does not accommodate them; there should be some balance of justice in a representative biographical narration.

Raghuji Shinde, Bhagoji Shinde

We have introduced Kashiram Shimpi and Appa Jagle in our previous narrations. There was one Raghuji Shinde living in Shirdi who became close to Baba, even before Baijabai came to provide bread and food to young Baba. Raghuji Shinde's aunt was a resident of Shirdi. Her son Ganpat Kanade (then aged thirty-five) was suffering from leprosy and fever. Baba gave him medicine, which contained cobra poison. Total abstinence from sexual activity had to be observed for the positive results of this medicine. Ganpat got relief from it for some time. However, he lost his life due to contrary behaviour and indulgence in sex. Such instances forced Baba to refrain from giving medicines. He thereafter used holy ashes as medicine. Bhagoji (brother of Raghuji) had similar fever. He had to be treated with hot iron bar burns on his back and cheeks. Bhagoji was saved from the disease as well as death. These events occurred after Baba's second arrival in Shirdi. Administration of uncommon medicines was later given up by Baba. Thereafter he moved over to divine methods and gave only udi and his blessings to the diseased.

Chandrabhan Seth and Khushalchand Seth of Rahata Village

Baba visited Rahata many times after the year 1858. Some people say that Baba stayed in an old, ruined Chawdi in Rahata for some time. A saintly person named Akbar Ali also stayed there with him. Baba's visit to Neemgaon to meet Nanasaheb Dengle and to Rahata to see Chandrabhan Seth and Khushalchand Seth is well-known to Sai devotees who have read *Sai Satcharitra*.

Sai Baba and Gadge Maharaj

The early days of Marathi saint Gadge Maharaj (who was also a social reformer) were similar to Sai Baba's unknown days and his early life. It is said that a fakir had asked for roti from Debuji (young Gadge Maharaj) while he was serving with his employer. He went home and brought roti for the fakir who was sitting under a tree near a forest. The fakir asked Debu whether he could give the former whatever he asked for. Debu said, 'I have no money but I can give you anything else.' The fakir asked for his life and had a long privacy with Debu in the forest and blessed him. Thereafter he was totally changed. He carried roti to the fakir once more. This time the fakir had filled a pitcher with water. He drank some of it and asked Debu to follow the suit. Debu went into trance. In later days, when the evolved saintly Gadge Maharaj came to Shirdi, Baba threw a brick at him, which left a crescent mark on his forehead. Baba said, 'You have eaten my flesh.' Gadge Maharaj became a realized soul. He reformed ignorant village people, pulled them out of superstitions, spread love for education, cleanliness, piety and honesty. The grace of the fakir made him a great social reformer and preacher in Maharashtra. This story was told by Nanasaheb Rasane, a devotee who served Sai Baba for twenty long years. This story cannot be fully believed because Gadge Maharaj's biographers have not made any mention of Sai Baba as his Guru. Historical confirmation can be accepted if biographies of both agree on the authenticity of the story. The unique and miraculous method of granting realization such as hanging the disciple upside down, giving a self-tested fruit to eat, throwing a stone and hurting the head to force a disciple into samadhi were adopted by Sufi saints like Baba Jan, Tajuddin Baba, Roshan Shah and others. The initiation of Gadge Maharaj conforms to this pattern. Sufi, Kabir and even Nath saints have adopted strange, miraculous methods of transformation of disciples or transmission of their own Guru power to the disciple. One can only conclude that the aulia or Siddha who graced young Gadge Maharaj was a representative of such great cult of murshid–*shagirda* (disciple) relationship as Sufi or Nath Gurus of old days.

Bapugir's Description of Young Sai

Bapugir has been mentioned earlier in connection with Chandorkar's experience at Jamner (Khandesh). Bapugir (or

Ramgir) Buva was a student in Shirdi School. If he had really seen Baba in his early days in Shirdi, his description of young Sai requires to be read with gravity of conviction. Bapugir has described Sai Baba's appearance as a young fakir whose hair touched his loins. His kafni was green in colour and his cap red. He held a staff in his hand and carried a chillum and matchbox with him. He used to sit below the neem tree in all seasons, irrespective of sunny or rainy days. The village children pelted stones at him and regarding him as a madman but Baba never broke his silence or composure.

Unity with Trinity of Datta

Many times Baba told the devotees who showed curiosity about his past that he was fostered on Mahur Gad. He stayed on bank of Ganges for eight years. He went to Girnar and Mount Abu and stayed at Akkalkot. He visited Daulatabad Fort, where Janardan Swami served him. Thereafter he reached Shirdi via Pandharpur. This account shows his unity with Datta incarnation like Shripad Vallabha. Baba was in fact the Dattatreya principle in human form. Sai devotees must inculcate in them that Baba was Lord Datta himself in his inner core.

The Guru Bandhu of Sakharam Maharaj

Megha was Baba's earlier formal pujari. Nana Jog hailed from Angaon-Kawad. When Guru puja started in Shirdi in 1909, Baba called Jog from Angaon-Kawad and asked him to stay in Shirdi for his puja. Nana Jog remembered that Baba had told him about Sakharam Maharaj (a Datta devotee–saint at Angaon-Kawad) who was his Guru *bandhu* (friend) and a co-disciple. Angaon was 4 miles away from Bhiwandi in Thane District. The mangoes of trees planted by Maharaj at Angaon were relished by Sai Baba. It is obvious that Sakharam Maharaj cannot be a friend and co-disciple of Sai Baba. It was a vogue in Baba's life to call the contemporary saints as the Guru bandhu. Similarly Gajanan Maharaj, Tembe Swami and such senior saints were held with utmost respect by Baba. Baba identified the Guru *tatwa* (element) in their incarnation. Shri Guru graced all masters and as such they came to be linked with Shripad Vallabha (Dattatreya). They were the disciples of his great Guru, and Baba was their Gurukul brother. Baba cherished the sentiment of love and bond of brotherhood for all living saints. Sakharam Maharaj was his faith brother in this strain. The relationship emanated from Dattatreya's identity.

Appa Jagle, Kashiram Shimpi, Waman Tatya

We have already seen that Mhalsapathi and his associates used to receive and render service to fakirs, mendicants, sadhus and vagrant men traversing the continent as pilgrims. Among those who did this service were Appa and Kashiram. There was also one person namely Waman Tatya who used to provide raw earthen pots to water the marigold and rose plants grown by Sai Baba in front of the Gurusthan. Baba's Guru service was unique and the love unparalleled. The pots were broken into pieces daily after watering, and new pots were provided every day. Waman Tatya has not been recorded in Baba's biography as very few came to know about this silent service to Baba and his Guru.

Devidas, Jankidas, Jawar Ali

The association of the great devotee saints like Devidas and Jankidas was available to residents of Shirdi in earlier years of Baba's stay in Shirdi village. The glory and greatness of Baba was felt by the rustic and uneducated villagers only through these benevolent men. The sadhus were renounced and dedicated and the stream of their life was sanctified by Baba's touch and proximity. Jawar Ali was a raw Muslim fakir who exerted influence on Baba and forced him to become his disciple. Jawar Ali took Baba to Rahata with him. It was through Devidas and Jankidas that Baba was brought back and settled in Shirdi after defeating Jawar Ali in a religious battle. Baba was far superior and fully evolved but he respected Jawar Ali and created a model of discipleship by his modest and servile behaviour. The story has been dealt with proper coverage in early parts of this biography and as such this has been cursorily mentioned here to commemorate the religious personalities like Devidas and Jankidas, who loved Baba and helped in spreading his glory. This chapter is dedicated to the unsung and forgotten association of some of Baba's early day comrades and admirers.

21

Memories of Baba's Early Days and Development of His Divinity

*E*very biographer has the tendency to pick up and touch upon some individuals and events of his choice and assign special importance to them in the narration. It is therefore possible that some personalities were overlooked and remained unmentioned. These narrations try to fix their place in Baba's running life story.

Baba Used to Sing and Dance

Baba, in his younger days, was fond of singing and dancing in ecstasy, reciting poems and songs by great saints of North. When wandering sadhus took a sojourn in Shirdi, he used to tie tiny bells to his feet and dance at the *Takia* (the song was Arabian and Persian worded). Baba indulged in this kind of excursion for twenty years from 1870 (when he settled in the masjid) to 1890, before he met Allah and reviewed his mission of life. Baba used to sing occult songs of Kabir. At the end of his mundane life in 1918, Baba arranged for qawwali concerts, samkirtans, reading of the Quran and *Hari Vijaya* just before he took his mahasamadhi. Chawdi in Shirdi became Baba's meeting place for newcomers, vagrant and saints in order to discuss religious and spiritual matters with them.

Rohilla and Nana Vali

Sai Baba's life story contains reference to one religious fanatic, Rohilla, who stayed with Baba for some time and practised his Muslim sadhana, reciting kalmas from the Quran at high pitch, acting violently with other devotees and exhibiting intolerance against Hindu and Islamic faith. Baba tolerated his eccentricities and belligerent behaviour with due regard. His behaviour is in contrast with that of Abdulla, the tolerant aspirant who arrived in Shirdi in 1890 and mixed with Hindu devotees with loyalty and tolerance. Nana Vali was another sadhaka with eccentric behaviour who had implicit faith in Baba. His strange antics caused anxiety and disquiet among other devotees around Baba, but Baba respected and tolerated him. Nana's samadhi has been built in Shirdi. He remains a part of Baba's spiritual aura. He once ordered Baba to stand up from his seat and himself sat there for some time. He then lovingly held Baba's hand and made him take his seat again. As he prostrated before Sai Baba, he confessed he had wanted to test Baba's powers as well as his humility at the time. Baba did not show his displeasure or fury at this act of Nana Vali. Thus Baba's humility was reaffirmed. No one dared again to examine his greatness as Nana did.

Baba was heard speaking several languages at night while he was in the Dwarkamai. The primary school teacher, Shyama, used to sleep in the neighbouring school building. He reported to have heard Baba speaking in Hindi, Urdu, English, Arabic and Parsi. These were Baba's earlier days in Shirdi, when visitors did not assume the later enormous flow and Baba's fame spread out in adjacent continents.

Music, Dance and Wrestling

It has already been stated that Baba used to sing Kabir's songs and dance with bells tied around his ankles. Many times, wandering singers, dancing troupes, qawwals and tamasha artist used to visit the mosque to present their talent before Baba. In last days of Baba's life, around 1917, the famous classical singer Alladia Khan visited Baba. This story would be retold in the last sequence of this biography.

Baba was also fond of wrestling. A devotee in Shirdi, who was Muslim, had a wrestler-cum-juggler son-in-law, named Mohiddin Tamboli. He used to sell betel nuts and talismans and Shirdi villagers respected him. One of his admirers was envious of Baba and challenged him to wrestle with Mohiddin. Baba readily accepted the challenge and lost the bout. He had agreed to go away from Shirdi if he lost the challenge. Accordingly he left the mosque for some days and retired to Lendi Baug. After that he donned the attire of a fakir and declared fakiri as the real Badshahi. This incident took place during Baba's early days in Shirdi.

Rohilla's and Nana Vali's stories are not so old. Especially, Rohilla's story was of initial days. Nana Vali was comparatively a later spiritual comrade of Baba (post 1890) and he seems to have seen Baba's later years of fame and glory. Meetings with Chandrabhan and Khushalchand Seth and Babasaheb and Nanasaheb Dengle were also from earlier episodes of 1860. Jawahar Ali, Jankidas and Devidas stories relate to very early day associations. Nanasaheb Dengle carried his devotion from these early days to the middle life days of 1890 and saw Baba's glory spreading around Maharashtra and India for a longer time. Readers must note this time frame.

In these early days of 1858–70 and 1870–90, Baba was recognized as a fakir or sadhu who came from an unknown region. The glory of Baba as a saint related to post-1890 era (i.e. 1890–1905) and his mahima as a Guru and incarnation spread by 1909, when men of knowledge and greater understanding and experience in spiritual sadhana came to occupy the galaxy of Baba's devotees in Shirdi environment. Other biographies of Sai Baba do not visualize the historical and chronological sequence of time showing the growth of his sainthood and Guruhood. We have, on the contrary, in his biographical narration revealed (i) the logical and chronological development of Baba's spiritual image; (ii) the beginning, growth and culmination of Baba's spiritual glory in the minds of the people in Maharashtra; and (iii) the stature and the higher position of Baba's avatarhood in Indian atmic galaxy and the global constellations.

We have been endeavouring to remove the discrepancies appearing in earlier biographies and to bring the undiscovered period and personalities to the fore, so that a realistic picture of the olden days of Shirdi is fully visualized by our Sai devotees and readers. The idea behind this effort is to show that the personalities associated with Sai Baba were not products of coincidence. They were like birds tied by a thread of Providence and brought in the proximity of Sai Baba, just as a Guru attracts his followers. Nana, Tatya, Bhau and Kaka whom Baba nicknamed with love have been great because of Baba's divine touch and nearness to them. Baba is the all-time Guru principle and we can even today establish relationship with him as Tatya, Bhau, Kaka and Nana to uplift ourselves to realized levels.

The Three Periods in Sai Story

As stated earlier we have divided this story in three segments: (1) The dusky early days (1870–90): Their social, historical and cultural backdrop and significance is unfolded; (2) Days of Baba's emergence as saint (1890–1905): The period is marked with appearance, stabilization and gradual development of Baba as saint and Chandorkar, Ganu, Abdulla, Dengle and Shyama as his devotee associates; (3) Manifestation of Baba as Guru (1909–18): The period declares Baba as an avatar of Guru and his epoch-making work for uplift of humanity and welfare of mankind.

The first part of the book depicts the personalities and events covering the first two segments of Baba's life. Thereafter we have decided to bring forth missing individuals from earlier periods as well as new personalities emerging in the third segment. The third segment itself is significant in as much as it brings the glory of Baba as an incarnation.

Hari Vinayak Sathe (Deputy Collector, Ahmednagar)

Sathe was a responsible officer of government who followed Chandorkar and Das Ganu and took his place in Shirdi galaxy. He was Deputy Collector of Ahmednagar and Settlement Officer in 1904. He was higher in rank and position compared to Chandorkar but Nana has been given more weightage and coverage in *Satcharitra*. Sathe had equipoise in sansara as well as religious matters. Megha, who became Baba's worshipper and Shiva devotee later, was a cook and a priest in Sathe's house. Sathe married the daughter of a Sai devotee, Kelkar, at the insistence of Sai Baba, for he was then a widower and had no male issue. Later he got a male child through Baba's grace. His name was permanently connected with Shirdi because of his construction of Sathe Wada near the Gurusthan for the use and service of devotees visiting Shirdi. He was a great Guru bhakta. Some persons have misrepresented him as a materialistic man but his service for the Sai devotees by constructing Bhakta Niwas at Shirdi cannot be forgotten. Sathe provided a great Shiva worshipper in the form of Megha who became immortal by his upasana and devotion for Baba as Lord Shiva. Baba wept at his death and bore all expenses of his funeral rights. He led Megha to Shiva abode. Sathe was witness to Megha's transformation as a devotee and loyal Shiva and Sai bhakta. He had made available Megha for Baba's worship as well as ritualistic upasana at Shirdi. At the beginning he had no spiritual aim, but Baba decided to attract, stabilize and develop Sathe as he wished. Sathe respected discipline and government rules and regulations. He was connected with Upasani Maharaj who was an eccentric sadhu and people in Shirdi disliked both. Baba made Sathe bring up a Dakshina Bhiksha-Sansthan and preside over the organization. The intention of this body was to reserve a part of daily dakshina which Baba doled out to individuals. The restriction on money doled out to recipients enraged the interested parties, who raised a hue and cry against Sathe and at the end the good work of Sathe was forgotten. It is said that violent beneficiaries like Nana Vali tried to attack Sathe with a club when he entered the masjid. Sathe was advised by his father-in-law, Kelkar, to leave Shirdi because of danger to his life. At last the great devotee had to leave Shirdi. However he had faith in Sai Baba till last. Narasimha Swami, biographer of the life of Sai Baba, has quoted about Sathe that he had full faith in Baba as the Vithal bhaktas have faith in Pandurang, although the Pandhari idol witnessed killing of the Peshwa Diwan right in front of it. The bhakti does not subside by unpleasant events. It thrives on calamities.

In the last paragraph we have stated how a Deputy Collector of Sathe's stature who was religious but practical and believed in rules could not get along in Shirdi when he tried to control and regulate the dakshina doled out by Baba at random and in munificent magnitude. The recipients were so fierce that they tried to harm Sathe and he had to leave Shirdi. Soon his financial status deteriorated and he had to sell his house and gold ornaments. Baba himself was pained when he came to know that Mrs Sathe, whom he regarded as his daughter, had to dispose all her ornaments. Sathe had printed and published stories heard from Baba's mouth in *Sai Katha Karandak*, which he collected arduously for the benefit of Baba's devotee worldwide. Readers are requested to appreciate the role and work of Sathe in the Sai Story. Both Sathe and Upasani were misunderstood and forced to alienate themselves from the holy Shirdi, one because of his discipline clashing against the greed of some souls and the other for his eccentricities which repulsed common devotees away from him.

We now discuss the relationship of Baba with men of position like Justice M.B. Rege, Pradhan, Tarkhad, etc. as they were part of Shirdi devotee circle by 1910 and had their position in Sai's life story distinctly marked. There were also personalities of spiritual value and background around Baba after 1910, such as Kushabhau, Upasani Dixit, Khaparde, Dabholkar, Narke and others. Bhishma, Radhakrishna, Chandorkar, etc. also have their parallel shadows over these days in the life story of Baba. Let us try to meet them in the next few chapters in their correct order, chronology and inner value because other biographies are bereft of this context.

22

Baba Graces Devotees in His Advanced Days

The first phase of Baba's physical sojourn at Shirdi (1905–09) was very significant in bringing forth his Guruhood. The later ten years were years of expansion of Guru bhaktas as well as Guru upasana on a larger scale and on a universal latitude befitting an avatar of the age.

We have discussed the advent of Radhakrishna Aai earlier chapter. Her devotion to Baba was a balance of devotion as well as the sansara of bhaktas in Shirdi. Sathe and Megha took care of Baba's puja and the accommodation of bhaktas in Shirdi. We would hereafter enumerate a few personalities of this period who were vital constituents to build up Sai upasana. We will also touch upon the nature of upasana prevalent at this juncture when Sathe, Megha and Kelkar were in the satsang or company of the Shirdi saint.

The devotees of Baba expanded after Radhakrishna Aai settled in Shirdi. Devotees from Bombay, Poona and other nearby cities came to Shirdi to see and experience the grace and love of Sai Baba, so as to transform their mundane life into divine by his touch and upadesh. The principled devotees, Guru aspirants and seekers of liberations also arrived. There were a number of householders who were tied by the bonds of material life and the maya of sansara who were trying to get relief at the hands of the

Guru avatar. Those who arrived in Shirdi gradually became part and parcel of the avataric life of Baba. Their arrival has not been recorded in the order of their year of coming, nor has the socio-political atmosphere prevailing in Shirdi and contemporary India been projected in logical order and chronological sequence by any earlier biographer of Sai Baba, including Dabholkar. The Hindu–Muslim devotees who arrived in Shirdi during 1905–18 were of very important stature and their understanding helps the readers to properly appreciate the evolution of devotion in Shirdi. But there are no resources available within contemporary or later writings about Baba. There were men like Nachne, Purandare, Dhumal, Dixit, Pradhan, Rege, Narke, Bhishma, Kushabhau, Thosar, Mahajani, Captain Hate, Buti, Khaparde, Upasani and Muslim visitors like Abdul Rangari, Nana Vali, Bade Baba, Chhote Khan, Adam Ali, Abdulla Jan, etc. Avasthe, V.B. Deo and many more were also closely related with Shirdi and its organizational built up. These educated, elite, simple, unassuming and multifaceted personalities formed a torrent of love in Shirdi till Baba's samadhi in 1918 and continued even thereafter. This was Lok-Ganga curling round the feet of our great epoch-making Guru avatar of Shirdi. We enumerate here few bhaktas who were near Baba during this period as an illustration. This is not an exhaustive list but only an exemplary or token projection of the then contemporary times to enable the readers to understand the context.

Rasne Is Graced by Baba

Shri Damushet Rasne was a merchant in Ahmednagar. His association with Baba was as old as that of Chandorkar. He was a materialistic man but had faith in Baba. According to his horoscope he had no chance of getting a progeny. However, Baba could surpass the evil conjunctions of inauspicious planets. He gave Rasne some mangoes and told him to 'die'. He got as many children as the mangoes numbered. During the Ram navami festivity in Shirdi, Rasne hoisted a flag for every progeny born to him. He even desired that Baba should be his partner in his business. But Baba warned him to keep Sai away money matters. Baba still loved the materialistic, mundane faith of Rasne and promised to help him even after his mahasamadhi. Damushet had continuous experience of Baba's presence and grace during his life.

Nachne's Materialistic Faith

He was another man who loved Baba but only for materialistic ends. He came in contact with Baba in 1909. Shantaram Nachne was a clerk in mamlatdar's office. Nachne harboured a faith that the sadhu who blessed him during his brother's operation was Sai Baba. He was saved many a time by Baba. Baba had materialized Nachne's transfer to Bandra Tehsildar office by prior suggestion. Baba accepted dakshina from this materialistic follower. Yet Sai Baba loved and helped him and others alike. Baba was not only glorious Guru for aspirants but also a friend to mundane men with worldly motives.

Raobahadur Dhumal

He was a renowned jurist in Nasik. He was associated with formation of sansthan around Baba's divinity. Dhumal made the rich Buti family approach the Shirdi saint. He was both mundane as well as religious. Baba looked after both these aspects. Dhumal had experience of Sai Baba being dynamic and active even after leaving his mortal body in Buti Mandir. Baba tried to create Guru loyalty and love in Dhumal. The congregational upasana in Shirdi was supported by Dhumal as an ardent follower of Baba. Baba used to guide Dhumal in his decisions. Many times he took decisions by throwing lots. When Dhumal's wife died, Baba had allowed shraddha rites in Shirdi. He even told that she was granted a higher place (*sadgati*) with his grace. Dhumal saw Baba sitting by his side when he underwent a serious operation in 1912. Dhumal earned Baba's grace simultaneously in both fields whether at family level or spiritual and atmic plane.

The above examples are indicative of the fact that Baba did not forsake even mundane and materialistic bhaktas, ignoring their spiritual shortcomings. Baba helped his bhaktas both ways (family and religious areas). He helped his aspirant bhaktas rise spiritually.

There were different associates of Baba like Chandorkar, Dhumal and Sathe. There were also Bhishma, Kushabhau, Upasani, Dixit, Pradhan, Rege and Tarkhad. These devotees illumined the last ten years (1909–18) of Baba's life. The history of these bhaktas in the last phase is more eloquent and well known to the readers of *Sai Satcharitra* because the author visited Shirdi at that time. Here we shall cover few bhaktas who will remind readers that they were the models who pushed forward the missionary chariot of the Sai avatar. These people were as great as the jurist and legislative councillor Khaparde, Lokmanya Tilak, N.C. Kelkar, singer Alladia Khan and other men of action. The influence of Ganu, Chandorkar, Sathe, Jog, Dixit, Upasani, Bhishma and Kushabhau remained unabated during these years of illumination in Baba's biography. The persons around Baba appearing in his Dwarkamai Satsang were educated–uneducated, literate–illiterate, rustic–urban, unrefined–refined, materialistic–spiritualistic. The real lustre of Baba cannot be projected by delineating only the mundane congregation. We must turn to more refined, disciplined, elite and elevated souls selectively.

Puja and Seva of Sai Baba

Baba allowed Dengle, Mhalsapathi, Jog and Megha to perform his puja. The first arti was written by Madhav Adkar and sung by Tatyasaheb Nulkar. Bhagoji, a leper, was the first man to provide physical service to Baba's human frame. Shyama was the first comrade to take all liberties even when talking to a saint and avatar of Sai Baba's order. Baba indulged him and allowed his silly pranks. Shyama repented when Baba passed away for he realized his own petty-mindedness and the contrasting greatness and liberal outlook of Baba. Nana was at Pune when Guru puja began in Shirdi. He was transferred to Thane in 1915. When he finally retired from Government service, Baba took care of Nana by perpetually protecting him, teaching Geeta and its philosophy to him. He nurtured Nana's dhyana-bhakti of Geeta and raised him to higher consciousness and understanding. Dengle, Nana, Ganu, Bhishma, Kushabhau, Upasani were taught the glory of Guru principle and the way of Guru kripa was made open to them for their progress and spiritual uplift. Megha's bhakti was rewarded with a vision and gift of trident and daily puja of Baba's form. Ganu's duality was removed and he was equipoised in dhyana, bhakti, yoga and karma. Ganu was taught the meaning and purport of the Upanishads. Even Kakasaheb's maidservant could give an example of Ishavashya teachings of balanced indulgence and renunciation.

Guru Bhakti of Kakasaheb Dixit

Solicitor Kakasaheb Dixit, a pure vegetarian Gujarati Brahmin, became part and parcel of Shirdi galaxy from 1907–08 along with other luminescent Guru worshippers. Upasani was late in coming (1911). Together they caused Shirdi Guru upasana to assume true shape and larger proportions. Kaka's aura of material importance was shining. As his leg was injured he was slightly incapacitated. He turned to Sai with a wish to strengthen his mind, knowledge and soul against susceptible body. Baba tested him on very many occasions till he finally stabilized himself as a true Guru bhakta. He brought Annasaheb Dabholkar, author of the famous *Sai Satcharitra*, to Shirdi in his own wake. Kaka devoted his self at the hands of Baba's grace. Baba had promised to carry him to heaven in a plane. A neem twig and the rooftop of the Dwarkamai fell down when Kaka left the world.

Bhishma and Sagunopasana

Bhishma was another Guru bhakta who arrived in Shirdi by the time Kakasaheb Dixit came. Baba recognized his Guru vision of Satchitananda. He attracted Bhishma to his Guru's feet. He was a learned man. He was also an adept composer and poet who delivered sermons and kirtans. Baba inspired him to write five poems on his Guru aspect as Satchitananda. He composed Sagunopasana for Baba's daily arti, adapting abhangas on Vithal, poems of Adkar, Ganu, Upasani and traditional slokas. The booklet was printed by Dixit. *Sagunopasana* thus became a daily upasana channel in book form. Baba gave a rewarding vision of atma to Bhishma and fulfilled his yearning for higher spiritual experiences.

Kushabhau and Dattopasana

Kushabhau was another Guru Datta devotee from Ahmednagar. He had some siddhis and tantric capabilities even before he stepped in Shirdi, because of his Dattatreya upasana of past. He was a dhyani who used mantra, tantra, abhichar and spirit power to help devotees, but Baba denounced such practices. Baba, being pleased by his allegiance, rewarded him with a boon to create ashes by waving his hand. Baba got Kushabhau married and he led a householder life in later years. Dabholkar, Khaparde, Tarkhad, Hate, Upasani soon followed Kushabhau and appeared in Shirdi. Thus there was a sequence of dhyani bhaktas, Guru worshippers and knowledgeable visitors.

Sai Baba's Congregational Upasana

The upasana of Baba as Guru started for the highly advanced Guru bhaktas in 1909, whereas the Sagunopasana of Sai Baba started much earlier in 1906 for the common devotee of prapanch household type. The first was on account of Radhakrishna, Bhishma and others. The other higher upasana came through Dixit, Kushabhau, Sathe, Upasani, etc. The congregational arti, rath processions, palanquins, illuminations, blowing of conchs and beating of drums were part of group *aradhana* (worship). The silent japa, dhyana, anusandhana was part of higher Guru cult. The group upasana was most popular because common artha-artharthi and distressed men and women came to Shirdi in large numbers, demanding all kinds of boons and reliefs from Baba. The procession and Chawdi festivity was notable with all kinds of fireworks, music, jayjaykar (hailing), chopdar, bhaldar, abdagirs and flags fluttering aloft. The prasad was distributed after the arti. When Baba returned from the procession he was anointed with saffron and chandan on the forehead. Baba was adored with sixteen upacharas. Baba's face was lit with divine light. His body was adorned with ornaments and garlands. When he stood before the Hanuman Temple, Chawdi and important places, he made occult signs which only the eight directions and nine stars could decipher. He smoked chillum and passed it among nearest devotees for a puff. The group upasana and high individual sadhana flourished hand in hand around the astounding divinity and glory that was Baba, the Eternal Guru. The Shirdi incarnation came down to unite religious faiths, sects and godheads. Thus both collective and individual Guru upasanas were the two wheels on which the avataric chariot of Baba moved to attract the attention of men and women to the mission for which Allah had stabilized him in Shirdi.

23

Distinguished Personalities in Shirdi Galaxy

*W*e have dealt with all significant men and women connected with Sai Baba in detail. There are also some people who are not vital to the story but have a mentionable role in Sai's life course. They are mentioned in the flow of the story to the extent relevant and are then forgotten or thrown in the background. We came in touch with such men and women in the previous two chapters and are continuing the same efforts in this chapter. Thereafter, we shall reintroduce our readers to the divine Guru aura of Sai from which we have veered far away. We shall also mention some Muslim devotees who have touched Baba's life in the last phase, predominantly beyond 1910. The concluding chapter in this segment will be on Baba's mahasamadhi. The story will not end there but a new segment will be opened to picturize those who led the torch lit by Baba.

The Ankita bhaktas of Sai Baba like Sathe and Dixit were dwelt upon in the preceding chapter. Here we shall dwell upon other Ankita bhaktas such as Mrs Tarkhad, Mr Galwankar, Mr Pradhan, Justice Rege, Prof. Narke, etc. These devotees find mention in other biographies but without proper balance of historical time sequence. While discussing them here, we are trying to impress an integrated picture of their place and role in Baba's life as far as it is possible with limited data in our hands.

Mrs Tarabai Tarkhad

The Tarkhad family came to know about Sai Baba through Mr Tarkhad's brother who was the Director of a Textile Mill. His daughter Nalini Tarkhad, who later became a renowned film star Nalini Jaywant, was then indisposed. Tarkhad respected saints and had experiences of saintly grace. He was convinced that Baba's lustrous eyes pierced through past, present and future. His divine knowledge read a man through and through. They knew that Baba was omniscient and omnipotent. His powers had protective shield. Baba did not preach yoga but removed obstacles in yogic practices. As we speak of Tarkhads, we shall speak of Prof. Narke, M.V. Pradhan, Galwankar, Kushabhau, Dixit, Justice Rege and Upasani Maharaj in course of our narrations. Touch of Baba not only transformed them but also filled them with splendour of illumination. Baba's life is a new lesson, new message and new edification to these devotees. These individual case studies deserve proper understanding and emphasis on Baba's life at this juncture in this biography because he manifested as Guru principle at this turning point.

Mr Galwankar

Raosaheb Galwankar came to Shirdi in later years (i.e. 1910–18) but his preparation for meeting such a godly saint started in his earlier births. Baba told his devotees, 'This man has come here today but I know him from past generations. His piety, honesty, morality was of such high order that I myself put him in the womb of his present mother.' There was a purpose for which Galwankar mustered himself into the Shirdi aura of Sai Baba. Rege was also of such great background. We devotees may not regret that we could not be contemporaries of Baba. Although we cannot be Reges, Galwankars, Upasanis, we can be with him even today. We can be Nana, Bhau, Tatya, Kaka even this day, if we foster companionship with Baba. Baba has no time limit. And we must imbibe in our mind that we are his dear ones and that he is our dear inner soul. The high sentiment of unity with Guru will launch us on Baba's 'sameepata' as well as 'salokya' bhakti platform. We must also have clear understanding that all who were physically near Baba cannot be best aspirants, devotees or evolved souls. They all had their shortcomings and imperfections. The only difference has been because of these persons' past merits. We have shortness of merit and this kept us a little away physically from Sai Baba's life. But even now, sadhana, dedication and love can rejoin us to Baba, crossing all borders of time and space. There is no barrier to our being Baba's Ankita bhaktas. Baba touches us with equal grace and uplifting compassion. Even saints meet practical-minded devotees in large numbers. They therefore thirst for spiritually inclined aspirants.

Galwankar was a man of character and morality. He was not asked to study Geeta, Bhagwat or Gurucharitra by Baba. But his love and thirst for Geeta and Bhagwat in his life had definitely got inspiration from the Shirdi saint. Galwankar visited Shirdi as late as in 1917. Baba put him in ecstasy by putting his graceful palm on his head. This was his greatness. Fourteen years after Baba's samadhi, Galwankar had a vision of Baba asking him to 'Ask for a boon' and Galwankar asked for 'Love'. Baba granted his prayer. Now Galwankar had gusts of love rising in his self. He gradually progressed under the guidance of his Shirdi master. Although physical nearness is prerequisite for bhakti, mental nearness is the real test for a timeless union.

Raobahadur M.W. Pradhan

Pradhan was an ideal devotee aspirant. He and his wife came to Shirdi in 1910 with the faith that Baba was the next parallel mahatma to be worshipped after Swami Samarth left his body. Sathe and Noolkar were present when Pradhan arrived in Shirdi. Baba welcomed them, accepted dakshina and a special feast of puran-poli offered by the Pradhans to devotees. Baba gave them the mantra 'Shri Ram, Jay Ram, Jay Jay Ram' and also alerted Pradhan regarding an impending paralytic attack on his mother. Baba sent them back home and cured Pradhan's mother in four days. Pradhan purchased the land occupied by Lendi Baug and offered it to Baba. Baba blessed Pradhan that he would always be by his side. Pradhan was promoted as Class II Magistrate by Baba's grace and was also elected as an MLA. Baba sent a hint about his mahasamadhi to Mrs Pradhan. He loved and held the Pradhans very dearly due to their spiritual merit and bond of past births. Baba gave his silver padukas to Mrs Pradhan. Narke, Rege, Tarkhad, Khaparde belong to special categories of devotees who came later in his life but had significant place with the advanced devotees. Mrs Tarkhad and Mrs Pradhan had many visionary messages from Baba. Baba convinced Mrs Tarkhad that the puja of his photo gives more peace of mind than their Prarthana Samaj prayers. To Pradhans, Baba gave experiences to the effect that he guarded their house and also protected them personally.

Justice M.B. Rege

Rege, an Ankita bhakta, was a spiritually progressed man even before he appeared in Baba's life. He had esteemed Baba as the creator, protector and vanquisher and an incarnation of unlimited spiritual power. Rege was an aspirant since his childhood. He used to sit in sadhana pose for hours, practise breath control and self-denial. He had an out-of-body experience when he was only twenty-one. He used to meditate on the Vishnu form of Baba. He had visions of Narayan with Baba sitting by his side. He saw Baba in his vision, when he had known nothing of Shirdi or Sai Baba. In some visions, Baba told him that he was indebted to Rege and he had come to have Rege's darshan. It suggested that Baba was Narayan himself whom Rege saw in his visions. He thus came to Shirdi with ideal and unmixed faith and devotion. Baba called him near and made him sit at his feet as a befitting honour to Rege's sadhana background. Rege enjoyed Baba's proximity for seven to eight years. He also associated with Radhakrishna Aai who was herself a yogini. Rege used to recite Baba's name. Baba advised others like Deo, Dixit, Chandorkar, etc. to read books like Geeta, Bhagwat, Ramayan, Dhyaneshwari. To Rege he said that books do not contain Brahma. He advised Rege to mould the heart and *buddhi* (knowledge) together and seat them in his bosom. This attracted grace. Gurushakti uplifts an Ankita aspirant who dedicates his mind, buddhi and ego at the feet of his Guru.

Mr Avasthi who was a judge in Gwalior was also brought to Shirdi by Rege in 1914. Avasthi had a lady yogini as his Guru. But his meeting with Baba did not hamper his devotion and loyalty to his Gurumata. Rege asked a boon from Baba that he should be near him in all his births. This was happily granted by Sai Baba. Baba used to say that Rege was at his feet and not at Indore. Baba and Rege both liked music. Baba liked songs sung by Rege. Rege knew very well that Baba did not want dakshina of money but that of mind, intellect, ego and soul. Rege used to contact Baba from where he sat. He knew that Sheelnath Maharaj (Devas), Madhavnath (Deogaon) and Tajjudin Baba (Nagpur) were not different from the self of Sai Baba. There was perpetual intercommunication among these great men.

Professor Narke

Narke was a highly educated professor who worked in an engineering college. Son-in-law of Shrimant Buti, he was an independent thinker, pragmatic, full of reasoning but still had an element of faith in Baba. His approach was that Baba's powers were not unlimited because he was encased in human body. Other devotees did not dare to hold such a view. Baba was always sportive and supported those who held such honest views, however correct or incorrect they may be. Persons of lower educational level became renowned devotees of Baba. But Prof. Narke's reasoning and rationalism came in the way of deep faith and devotion for Baba, although he came in Baba's fold in 1912. Narke visited Shirdi on account of Buti's insistence. He agreed to visit Shirdi only after Buti obtained formal consent of Baba. Narke's mother was also a follower of Baba. When Shyama introduced Narke to Baba, Baba said he had known Narke since past fifty births. Such were the bonds of generations which drew his devotees nearer him. Prof. Narke tried to analyse Baba's internal powers and omniscience through logical analysis and intellectual scanning. He fell short of ideal standard of faith and surrender.

Narke's analysis was that Baba's could see the past and the present. However, as for the future, one cannot fully observe its magnitude or direction. This is because the future turn of events and the shape of action and effect is always a varying factor. Narke became a Trustee of Shirdi after Butiwada was constructed in 1918. He remained jobless for thirteen months during Baba's association. He used to read advertisements for employment in Burma and Balaghat in newspapers. This was in 1915. He was tired of his unemployed status and desired to accept a kafani from Baba while the latter was distributing kafanis to some of his other devotees. Baba told him that he could not be given a kafani for his fakir did not permit it. Baba promised Narke's mother that he would fix her son in Poona. However, the advertisements placed always related to distant countries and not Poona. At last the Poona Engineering College vacancy came to be advertised in papers. Baba asked Narke to apply there. There were a number of candidates who had applied for that post in Poona. And while Narke had no acquaintance or influence, Baba used to assure him that Allah will give his blessing. And blessed he was, for he got the post.

Narke's children were short-lived. With Baba's blessings, Narke begot four children from 1918 to 1934. Baba had given up his body by then but the grace of Allah was operative. Events like this convinced the intellectualism and rationalism of Prof. Narke that although the future is not fully decided or fixed, a godly saint can shape it according to his wish. Baba told Narke that all resided in the entire universe. He admitted that Guru does nothing. He illumines the inner lustre, which is already present there inside a disciple. Further he advised Narke that one should remain dedicated. So, if he takes one step towards the Guru, the latter will take ten steps towards him. The Guru can help a disciple only if he has self-control and discrimination. Baba said that he was everybody's father and that there was no limit to what they, his children, could ask for from him. Did Narke comprehend the true meaning of Baba's words? Baba had clarified that even though an incarnation has human limits, there is no reason why the devotee should not ask or pray for their desires to be fulfilled according to what they deserved and what the human form of the avatar could grant them. The basis on which Narke's faith stood limited his own progress because he could not reach the height and depth of love and surrender, which Mhalsapathi, Dixit and Megha had achieved. Full surrender and faith can give an aspirant full measure of grace. Only untainted loyalty, implicit faith and consummate dedication could bring home liberation. The precious truth of sadhana could be learnt from Narke's episode here.

The Contemporaries of Baba and Their Role in Shirdi Galaxy

This list of small and big associates of Baba now comes to an end except for some Muslim devotees who need mention so as to give shape to the secular frame of Baba's devotee world. We had a special purpose to educate our readers how these men got forgotten but still hold important lesson in spiritual knowledge. Baba's life was a life of avatar or Guru. The power of Guru had descended from the cosmos to give a new vision, new philosophy and dimension to transform humanity through the laboratory of India, the Gurusthan of the world. The biographers had a special predilection for their friends, relatives or intimates and this has caused their writings a limit. The boundless brotherhood and followings had been the true characteristic of Sai avatar, but unfortunately writers limited their scope to Sai devotees they came across in Bombay city only. Some have publicized public men, whom they had chancily come across and coincidently had some respect for Baba, but had no value of sadhana, bhakti or penance to befit the galaxy of Sai devotees. The biographers of saints should find his real glory in the personalities who have illumined his life story or philosophy or who are vital to the spread of Baba's inner secularity, spirituality and mahima. This biography has set for itself special milestones of visionary experiences, search lights of dhyana, bhakti, karma and yoga which illumine human life and atmic stature. It is therefore unique and different. If the biographies are written with mundane values and intentions, the very basis and purpose of the saint's life mission will be fully thwarted and hijacked by inferior motives. The Guruhood of Baba was to lead humanity to light and this light must emerge from the biographies. *Sai Geetayan* appeals to the writers to sing the arti of God through their poetic and literary art as follows: 'Let us raise our voice to sing the arti of light.'

'Arti of light' means singing the glory of Guru or God through a eulogy. The great and immortal literature is to be couched in vibrant words and live phrases oozing Guru's divine grace and thrills of shakti. Such literature is eulogy of lustre. Such creations are modern Vedas and Upanishads. The writers are modern rishis graced by cosmic Guru. The words written by such authors raise human consciousness above mundane limits and make human awareness merge in cosmic awareness. Sanskrit language has used the word 'Prasadik' for such poetry or literary works.

24

Guru Purnima (1990) and Essence of Baba's Guru Mahima

*W*e have seen how Allah projected Baba after his command in 1886 to reveal himself as the Guru incarnation. This began to manifest between 1905 and 1909 and Baba was known as Satchitananda Guru, a roving incarnation of Dattatreya in Malanga fakir attire. Nana, Ganu, Sathe, Dixit, Dhumal, Bhishma, Kushabhau, Upasani and many others acted as catalytic agents in revealing Baba in the new form. They became the foundation stones and basic material of his cosmic mission as Guru. Baba was simultaneously helping sansaric, mayic and materialistic men and women who had faith in him to develop as bhaktas surmounting their shortcomings and foibles. The Guru Purnima of 1909 was the selected hour for this recognition and manifestation. This was a glorious period of Guru mahima of Baba.

Baba's mission did not end with his mahasamadhi. It marked the expansion of his power, glory and dynamic capacity. It was his entry into the universal plane to lead his work more comprehensibly and more conclusively. We have not given so much emphasis on individuals in the brighter segment of his life (1909–18) because they are more commonly and extensively known and studied by readers with the help of other books and authors. On the contrary we have concentrated extensively on the earlier unknown period (1835–1905), which is more obscure and incomprehensible for lack of contemporary data.

Guru Purnima in Shirdi

The festival of Guru Purnima started in Shirdi in 1909 and went on to become a regular feature. In fact the Guru lovers had assembled earlier in 1908 to have Baba's darshan and upadesh. However, Baba was in trance (*yoga nidra*) then. Bhaktas sang the morning raag of Bhupali:

> 'O Shripati, Shrikanta, rise up from slumber.
> If you are yourself in slumber, who will rouse the sleeping sansara?'

When Baba woke up, he told his bhaktas, 'You have come together on this auspicious day. But I am not God. I am his servant. God dwells in the sky occupied by Brahma and operates even from a pole, like this pole in Dwarka. You adore this pole, which symbolizes my fakir Guru. Guru is not an image or figure. He is a principle.' In 1908, Baba made all Guru bhaktas worship the pole against which he leaned in the masjid. Next year onwards he allowed them to worship his feet. Baba's devotees told him that he was their Guru idol and so asked him to give them mantra or upadesh. They wanted him to rekindle their hearts with the flame of his own heart. Baba was pleased. He told them that dedication and surrender to one's Guru was the secret of bhakti. The Nath, Datta, Sufi and Kabir cult have respected the Guru–disciple relationship with utmost value. Meditation on Guru form will transform a bhakta into Guru just as a moth which concentrates on a bee and becomes the bee itself. Baba's message, 'You look to me. I shall look to you,' is the essence of secret of Guru marga. He said, 'My Guru taught this to me. He never imparted any mantra to me. He carried my weight on his shoulder and also protected me from all sides. I had only to look at his face. Shraddha and saburi were the two things he took as dakshina from his disciples. I served my Guru for twelve years. What I am before your naked eyes is itself a sakshatkar. One who was Rama and Krishna is now Sai. I shall carry you beyond the waves of maya by my own power of grace and compassion. You must hold fast my hand at the very beginning. You cannot progress without my help, irrespective of whether you practise yoga, karma, dhyana or bhakti. The final stage will only be reached if you hold fast my hand and walk as I direct.'

Baba's Message to the Guru Bhaktas

'Break the wall of ego. This is coming in our way. You are mine and I am yours. This is my mantra. Shastras and Vedas are at my feet. When your heart is clean and actions are pure, I will appear to hold the reins of your life chariot. I will lead your life vessel. Leave "I" consciousness and ego as doer, and you will be fit to carry on my avatar's work and mission divine to transform the world into welfare of self and uplift of human birth. The Guru made a revolutionary change in me. I surrendered my body, mind, intellect and ego at his feet and he transformed me into Satchitananda. Even when you are on the stage of life connect yourself to the Guru and change the course of life into liberation.'

The Coconut from Datta Saint

Pundalikrao Nandedkar, a lawyer in Marathwada, was given a coconut with his obeisance by Datta saint Vasudevananda Saraswati for presenting it to Sai Baba. Pundalikrao took the coconut with him during his visit to Shirdi but during the journey his friends broke the coconut and mixed it in *chiwda* (savoury) and ate it inadvertently. When Pundalikrao reached Shirdi and met Baba, he unmistakingly asked for the gift from his brother. Pundalikrao was puzzled. When asked again about the coconut, he pleaded forgiveness for it was lost. He promised to compensate it by another coconut. Baba was enraged and told him, 'No coconut even made up of gold and silver can equal my brother's coconut.' For Vasudevananda was Dattatreya himself and his gift cannot be equalled by anything else. He believed that anything given must reach its destination. He was extremely grieved that his brother's wish was not fulfilled as the coconut did not physically reach him.

Change in the Rules of Destiny

Shyama mostly acted as an agent of demanding devotees and importuned Baba to grant unjust favours to them, which were rejected by destiny. Though Baba loved Shyama, he resented the fact that he could not cross the lines of destiny. But Shyama insisted for favours and Baba granted boons—children to childless, health to the diseased, fortune to the distressed, and relief to the agonised. Baba explained to Shyama that the karmas were responsible for such sufferings and no interference was warranted therein. But he finally yielded to Shyama and granted favours improper and undeserving to men and women. This increased superstitious beliefs and unruly behaviour. Baba felt that this was misuse of siddha powers, for the Siddhas have to suffer the prarabdha themselves to give relief to the wanting persons. The karmas do not recede of their own accord.

Ganu Comments on Ishavashya

Once while interpreting the *Ishavashya Upanishad*, Ganu could not construe the meaning of, 'Tyen tyakten bhunjitha (enjoy the pleasures in a renounced state).' Baba told Ganu that Dixit's maidservant would explain this Vedanta to him. Thus Ganu went to Dixit's house, where he heard a young woman singing about her yearning for a costly sari. Ganu was moved. He asked Dixit to present her a sari. The maid was happy to get the sari. Next day again Ganu found her singing the same song, but the plaintive tone had vanished from her. Why did she sound happy even when she wasn't wearing the sari? This was because she knew she possessed the sari, even if she wasn't wearing it then.

We are part of God, and God permeates the universe. He is the possessor of all objects. Hence we are also possessors of all objects. We must not pine for what we do not get nor grieve for what we have abandoned. This attitude teaches detachment in enjoyment and satisfaction in abandonment. This was the essence of *Ishavashya Upanishad*. The meaning in brief is that human beings are part and parcels of God—the Master of universe. We are also masters of his universal wealth. We must learn to react to the pleasures of the world without indulgence. We must also learn to abandon pleasures or possessions without regrets or agony of parting them. This in fact is balanced attitude to the loss or gain in life.

Visit of Tilak and Alladia Khan (1915–17)

From 1910 onwards a number of Muslim devotees arrived to see Baba. Among them were Bade Baba, Chhote Khan, Rohilla, Abdul Rangari, Adam Ali and Abdulla Jan. There were also Hindu devotees like Narke, Deo, Khaparde, Galwankar, Tarkhad and Pradhan who were of a high educational and social order. We cannot give justice to each one of them in proper measure as the information available about them is broken, incomplete and sporadic. The sadhana of the people of Muslim origin has not been explored much by biographers of Sai Baba. However, a reference to few great personalities of the contemporary days visiting the Dwarkamai is must here. Before Tilak arrived in 1917 and classical singer Alladia Khan in 1915, many others had been visitors of the saintly abode. Dabholkar arrived in 1909, Tarkhad, Nulkar, Khaparde came in 1910 and Upasani in 1911. Purandare visited Shirdi in 1912, Narke came in 1913. Dabholkar was a magistrate, an expert in shastras and fit to write ovimetre biography. However, he was squabbling about the utility of Guru during his first visit to Shirdi, when Baba intervened and called him Hemadpant. This bridled his analytic and searching mind and he became a devout and surrendered pen-man. Unfortunately his biography does not record events of Baba's life in a logical or chronological sequence. Narasimha Swami was a better—logical—writer. Khaparde was a jurist counsellor, orator and learned man who observed Baba's daily life and kept a diary of events during 1910–11. Swami Sharananand and Khaparde recorded many unknown day-to-day events in Baba's life. The comparison exposes the limits of Dabholkar's writings. Upasani was a golden leaf in Baba's life. He was cultivated into a Siddha by Baba's grace which kept him away in Khandoba Temple. Upasani adopted Vedic and orthodox ways instead of secular ways of Sai Baba. He started his ashram in Sakori (3 kms away from Shirdi) and went the other way, leaving the universal mission of unity started by Baba. The great vocal singer Alladia Khan arrived in Shirdi and satiated Baba's ears with his classical bhakti sangeet in 1915. Tilak arrived in Shirdi with Khaparde and N.C. Kelkar in 1917 and paid homage to Baba, who asked him to retire from politics. The new era in politics was to start with peace and non-violence and Tilak had to keep away from active politics to concentrate more on his ultimate spiritual welfare as Baba foresaw that it was the last phase of his life.

Sai Is Inner Soul of Beings

Baba, who protected prapanch and paramarth of devotees, was not operating for human beings alone. He would know the pain and agony of the entire living world including birds, animals and plantation. Once Baba called for bread from Laxmi because he felt hungry. Though Laxmi knew Baba had finished his meal just a little while ago, she obeyed his orders and brought freshly prepared bread. Baba kept it before an emaciated dog at the door of the mosque. When the dog ate the bread, Baba's hunger vanished. Laxmi was enraged because Baba, instead of eating the bread himself, gave it to the dog. Baba consoled her saying that he ate through the mouths of all creatures. He did not live in the 5½-foot human frame. The entire world was his body. He lived in every heart. He saw through all eyes. He was the thousand-headed Purusha of cosmic form.

Baba's Interaction with Devotees

Baba eradicated the agony of distressed with his divine powers. He instilled faith in those who adored a particular deity by giving them her darshan. The aspirants were encouraged by Baba to meditate, to have human compassion and to serve mankind as God. Ordinary devotees were asked to recite the names of godhead. All names and forms were his own and merged in his divinity as universal Guru or God. The grace came through deep devotion and faith. He wanted his followers to surrender their mind, buddhi and ego at the feet of Guru. He used to protect high aspirants from being entangled in karmas that bind them in the fetters of fate. Baba told that selfless renounced life was sufficient for Mhalsapathi's *mukti* (salvation). He also enjoined dhyana-bhakti and unattached approach of Geeta to Nana. Pure emotion and intense devotion was not only adequate but fully rewarding to Megha. The same Baba wanted Upasani's highly evolved soul to burn his karmadasha, by constant acid-tests and purification of his personality. Upasani's mind was dormant with 'paapa purush' and 'punya purush' (good and evil qualities) simultaneously. Ganu's capacity to flood his audiences with the flow of devotion and dhyana edified them with the light of the spirit leading him to liberation. It was essential for everybody to kindle the flame of atma by constant dhyana of Guru form. When a devotee reached the Bhav-avastha by yoga, he had to surrender to Baba (the eternal Guru) for the flow of liberating moha kripa. Grace alone helps to lift the aspirant to turiya and later unmana. He was ready to grant higher stages to higher aspirants through love, chintana and dedication. This was the secret of his kripa. Baba's kripa was manifold and multifaceted.

Baba Was Ananda

Sai Baba was Atmananda personified, for he had come as an avatar on earth to fulfil the mission of Allah. His devotees did not require mantra, tantra, pothi, pilgrimage, fasting, rituals and study of love because he himself was the final destination to be sought (Satchitananda). He was love, truth, ananda.

Baba said:

'I am the fragrance of Sahashradal Lotus.
I am the vibrant shakti and ambrosial grace.
I am unlimited bliss and ecstasy myself.
I am the Omkar which you have to hold fast to enter the astral void.'

(*Sai Geetayan*)

If a sadhaka meditated on Baba's form, he would light the lamp of his heart.

Baba also said:

'I am the astounding point where prana merged in the mind.
I am the anahata sound with the musical vibrations.

I am the chaitanya, flame of light (jyoti).
Hold fast my hand and taste the amrita of mukti.'

(*Sai Geetayan*)

Baba's work was to merge the surrendered soul in atmic knowledge to open doors of dhyana, *prem* (love) and *satya* (truth)—the final destination of human birth. This is the essence of understanding moksha.

25

Purandare's Devotion, Upasani Maharaja's Disciplehood and Association of Some Muslim Bhaktas

𝓑aba attracted Abdulla, Ganu and Chandorkar to Shirdi to create suitable atmosphere for the manifestation of his new incarnation and spread the celestial light of his Guruhood for uplifting the distressed and ignorant masses among various conflicting religious sects. We have scanned devotees of Baba consisting of small and big, learned and ignorant, lowly and elite men and women within his fold. Materialistic followers like Nachane and Rasne, advanced and knowledgeable personalities like Nana and Ganu, evolved and aspirant souls like Bhishma, Kushabhau and Upasani, dedicated and surrendered effigies like Justice Rege, Pradhan, Tarkhad and Galwankar, as well as cautious, rationalist and analytic-minded Professor Narke. Let us now examine two opposites like Purandare, who was materialistic and a passionate lover of Baba, as against highly spiritual and realized devotee of Upasani's stature.

R.B. Purandare and His Allegiance to Baba

Purandare was an ordinary clerk with meagre income. He was as materialistic as Rasne and Nachane but had deep love and faith in

Baba. His love and allegiance was so impassioned that he would sacrifice his self to keep loyalty with his object of faith. His sentiment of bhakti was as deep as that of Baija, Tatya, Abdulla and Radhakrishna Aai. Some of Baba's learned devotees cannot stand in comparison with Purandare due to their one-pointed faith and loyalty to Sai. Saints do not pant for your knowledge or learning, they thirst for untainted devotion and uncompromising love the devotee cherishes for them and the unequalled loyalty which lies deeply entrenched in his bosom. Purandare was moved by Ganu's kirtan and firmly decided that Sai Baba was his destined Guru. He immediately visited Shirdi with his ailing son, who was cured by Baba. His love and loyalty was stabilized. Baba told Purandare that he was protecting him since his childhood. The bhakta was entwined in Baba's love and served him. He endured Baba's fits of fury and love. He helped to control the Ram navami mob crowding at Shirdi. Baba made him build a house at Bandra within his limited means. In his miraculous ways, Baba cured his wife from fatal ailments. Purandare's faith became stronger. Baba was his God. Whenever Baba fell ill he waited for Purandare to come and serve him. Purandare's love, faith and loyalty won Baba's heart. He was not an aspirant like Rege, Bhishma, Upasani but he was still dearer and nearer to Sai Baba. His love and loyalty could withstand the acid test of any sacrifice. Baba rewarded this simple, materialistic man in ample measure.

Kashinath Upasani Maharaj

Baba attempted to carve a true disciple out of Kashinath Upasani who was a learned pandit, poet, yogi and dhyani. He had contracted asthma due to some wrong yogic practices. He was an ayurvedic physician, who was responsible for the death of some of his patients due to wrong administration of medicines. Thus he had to leave his profession and abscond. He renounced prapanch due to misfortune and ill destiny, and became an eccentric sadhu. He was attracted to Baba. Baba purified him and gave him experiences of the entire universe and galaxies dormant in his self. However Upasani did not carry Baba's secular mission further, for he was fond of Vedic yajnas and upasanas.

Sufi Influence

That Sai Baba's spiritual family includes mainly Hindu bhaktas cannot be denied. His spiritual frame was formed through the occult and miraculous touch of his murshid of aulia sadhana style, which showered grace munificently by mere touch or such symbolic act of grace. His first experience was of Tajuddin, Haji Malang or Khwaja Garih Navaz style. The act of grace could be hanging upside down, being offered a fruit tasted by murshid, being hit with a stone or piece of brick on the forehead. This was actually the transmission of Guru's power into the disciple and force his consciousness in spiritual ecstasy of samadhi state. The body consciousness is driven out and knowledge gradually filled in. This is parallel to shaktipath in Guru Datta's Kundalini yoga. The flame merges in flame. Guru transforms disciple into divine consciousness.

Muslim Influence

Baba's first experience in sadhana was essentially Kabir or Sufi style. It was the fakir Guru who gave him the experience of supreme bliss. He remembered throughout his life his Guru at the Gurusthan or fakir in the masjid. However his further sadhana under Vaishnava saint Venkusha filled the supreme and colossal experience into yogic samadhi, grace of Lord Dattatreya and the dhyana, bhakti, yoga framework. It was an all-pervading cosmic assimilation which all dharmas and sadhanas aim at and covet as the final state of universal consciousness or being. Baba therefore could not be separated from the word 'Allah' and fakir origin. He was dressed in a fakir attire in the early teenage days when he came to Shirdi. A cap, pyjama zabba and then kafani and a knot of cloth on the head. The tinpot and the sataka followed. He looked like a Sufi–Kabir sect sadhu or a Hindu mendicant siddha. He was therefore received as such when he stood before the Khandoba Temple. He was taken to be an idol-breaker by Mhalsapathi. The biographers of Baba have taken note of Sai Baba's outward appearance only. As for his inward Muslim style sadhana background and ties with Muslim mujawar, they are ignorant and therefore silent. The mention of Abdulla, Rohilla and other personalities of Muslim cult who came to Shirdi in later years have been cursorily mentioned in course of narration. In fact the figure of fakir, the masjid and Allah's name had deep impression on Baba. He could see them and could contact them every moment. The influence grew because of his stay in Fakir Roshan Shah's house for twelve long years. His language, lifestyle and behaviour were stamped with Muslim impact. It was therefore that Muslims were more attracted towards his lifestyle. However, his love and equal treatment of Hindu gods, Hindu upasanas kept Muslims at a distance from him. Hindus are naturally tolerant, and hence accepted his Allah and fakiri along with Ram, Krishna, Shiva and Guru Dattatreya. Baba had mastered the Quran but Muslims were not seen studying either the Quran or practicing Muslim sadhana in Baba's presence and guidance. Only Abdulla took the benefit. He was a single model of secular tolerance among the outnumbering Hindu devotees. It was only in 1890 that he came to Shirdi due to intervention of his murshid from Nanded and stabilized himself around Baba, practicing his Muslim ways of worship and adoration.

The Period of Flow of Bhaktas

The period 1892 to 1910 was marked with the arrival of several Hindu bhaktas from all over Maharashtra, adjacent states and India as a whole. But the period does not record any Muslim bhaktas of significance coming to Shirdi and laying their mark on Sai Baba's life. This does not mean that no Muslim, Christian or Parsi bhaktas visited Shirdi. Among Muslim devotees who did approach Baba, very few could even understand and appreciate the impact of the great Master like Roshan Shah Fakir had left on Baba's spiritual make-up and aura. They should have known this and made efforts to benefit themselves from the Kabir–Sufi sadhana and process of mercy and grace Baba stood for. The fakir Banne Mia and Shamsuddin of Aurangabad had deeper contact with Baba from their Aurangabad abodes. No Muslim could learn from these bonds of atmic relationships. Baba's way of ecstasy which he had been gifted by his Guru was unique. These devotees could have changed the colour of their life and spirituality by the association and companionship of Sai Baba which was readily at hand. The later period mentions persons like Fakir Darvesh Shah, Chhote Khan, Anwar Khan, Maddu Shah, Irus Shah, Abdul Rangari, Adam Ali, Abdulla Jan and others. They have been cursorily enlisted by Baba's biographers but they seem to have been forgotten long ago because they could leave no lasting impression on the Shirdi environment. These persons had come later than 1910 and should have been more impressive due to Baba's rising glory after 1905–09, when he was known to be an avowed Guru and an incarnation.

Anal Haq

Sufi saints used to declare Anal Haq (I am God), which means Aham Brahmasmi (I am Brahma), when they attained higher state of consciousness. Sufis merged their human ego in Allah's super consciousness. This is their higher experience. All sadhana is for being one with Guru. Guru pervades the existence of the disciple and makes him part and parcel of God. Baba's treasure was the fakir under the neem tree. He directed Baba to do everything. On his asking Baba demanded dakshina from the devotee. The Sufi and Muslim saints or contemporaries of Baba like Tajuddin, Haji Malang and others had similar grace experiences from their murshids. The Guru–disciple relationship was their strength. The Hindu disciple also followed surrender and dedication to Guru with unmixed devotion and implicit faith. This Hindu style devotion was learnt by Baba from his Vaishnava Guru, Venkusha with whom he had stayed for six years. Baba came to Shirdi with the light and illumination of this sadhana. When he finally settled in Shirdi in 1858, he was both fakir as well as Datta. He was Ram, Rahim and Allah simultaneously. The message of unity of Hindus and Muslims was his heritage right from his Kabir birth to Sai birth. The miraculous, occult and great mysterious coordination was the characteristic of Sai avatar. We have picturized Baba with proper coordination and unity of these two major religions at length because the depiction of Baba without the essential data will present his one-sided picture.

Fakir in Masjid

The fakir in the mosque was Baba's father. He was the protector, uplifter, fosterer of all. He was omniscient, omnipotent God. He ruled over time, space and directions. The village celebrated Ram navami 1911onwards and sandal procession as well as bands, trumpets, cymbals sounded or flags held aloft in masjid with Chawris, abdagirs also held high. Baba sometimes called the masjid as Brahma mosque. The fakir ruling, it would lead all by white path. It was also called the Dwarka of Krishna. However, this unity of sects and religions was not appreciated by rustic, uneducated masses. Only some educated man of foresight knew the secret of this secularity, although common Muslim man was drawn to Baba due to his powers and glory. They did not settle there in full faith for long. No Hindu or Muslim ever reached Baba's spiritual height. It is therefore that Baba said all were his devotees, nobody was his disciple. This was a disappointment in reality. Even the phrase or title bhakta is wrought with tests. There would be a few and far in between who climbed the devotee step and reached sufficient height or level. If we see the picture of devotees, we come across a contrast showing a perfect master against imperfect followers. This may sound strange to a common reader, but it is a stark factuality. Nobody reached the state of disciple, nay, even bhakta qualification. These are high tests of merit.

Chhote Khan's Association

Chhote Khan came to Baba in 1910 due to financial problems. Baba rejected him first due to his bad past, but later helped him. He came four times for money from Vaijapur. There were two Muslims, namely, Shaikh Abdulla and Abbas Shaikh who acquired siddhis from Sai Baba. These were Sufi-style instant transformations worked out by Sai Baba. Anwar Khan was a Muslim who was tired of life. Baba made him read the first chapter of the Quran and helped him complete Haj pilgrimage. He had to read the Quran at midnight to fulfil his longings.

Kazi Anwar from Ahmednagar

Kazi Anwar wanted money for building a mosque. Baba helped him find underground treasure from which the work was carried out. Such help and miracles are common factors in the life of Sufi saints. This gives us a clear idea of Baba's Sufi sainthood. This we emphasize here so that the readers remember this important Sufi link of miracles.

Rajab Ali Mohammad

Rajab was not spiritually prepared and as such Baba did not desire to bless him. However, he asked from Baba nothing but peace and salvation. He was in the company of Baba Jan and Tajuddin Baba. The company of such great saints brought home to him a way for evolution of his soul by satsang.

Abdul Rangari (Thana), Adam Ali (Bandra) and Abdulla Jan (Korhala)

Rangari's wife had pain and swelling in her throat. Baba cured her with udi. Abdul Rahim Rangari danced in ecstatic state and sang songs of love for God. Baba liked his Sufi way and joined him to his spiritual destination by reviving this Sufi sadhana. Baba's sadhana was also Sufi in the beginning. He had bhakti, dhyana, sadhana as a sequel in his earlier sadhanas.

Adam Ali was an estate broker at Bandra. He was short of funds at the time of the marriages of his sons and daughters. Baba blessed him with munificent gains as broker, whenever he visited Shirdi for help. He did not progress much beyond his material needs. Rangari also did not crave beyond monetary benefits.

Abdulla Jan of Korhala was a different type. He was Peshawari pathan. He came to Baba when he was still young. Baba removed his intolerance and apathy for Hindu devotees. He promised Abdulla Jan that he would teach and reform persons even after his samadhi. Abdulla believed in performing timely and regular namaz, feeding people, Ramzan fasts and giving *daan* (doles) to poor. Baba supported his way of thinking, although Baba never believed in rituals and was above all karmic exercises. He was not only a perfect Muslim but also a perfect Hindu. The rituals and rites are not essential to Siddhas and Masters because they do not believe in extremism. Baba was perfect. Only imperfect and raw aspirants require the fast, bath, 'dos and donts' disciplines. Baba knew the heart of every religion and every philosophy. He was not bound by mechanical ways of blind religious fanatics. The influence of Muslim persons and ways in Shirdi has been dwelt upon here to show that Baba stood for all religions alike and was Master and Guru for all sects and creeds. He was Allah or God incarnate. He was worthy of adoration by all religions and sects.

We have already discussed Abdulla's advanced role in Shirdi precincts. Baba fructified his service and told him that he had been taken across the sea of sansara. His *matti* (earth) had been turned into gold. 'What a big edifice has been constructed?' This shows that Baba gave him high state of progress. Although he did not become a saint, he was purified, his life was cleansed and he was led to higher level of evolution. His birth was made fruitful, giving him scope for higher upliftment in future births.

Perfect Blend of All Philosophies and Sadhanas

Baba's perfect assimilation of all religions was so convincing that Hindus treated him as Hindu God and Muslims looked upon him as Allah. But the impact of Muslim style was deeply embossed in his early day make-up, which men of insight could vividly visualize. Baba never expressed any bias to one religion because he represented universal religion, common to all and acceptable to mankind as a whole. The differences exist with only imperfect men and women.

26

Baba Decides to Merge in His Cosmic Form!

*L*et us now wind up the analysis of devotee world of Baba, which we have attempted so far and describe the mahasamadhi of Baba. We shall discuss here a few remaining devotees like Nimonkar, Mankar, Capt. Hate, Nulkar, Sagun Naik, Bapsaheb Jog, Mahajani, Khaparde and B.V. Deo.

Some Bhaktas of Baba

In the residuary list of contemporary bhaktas, we have Balasaheb Bhate who was mamlatdar at Kopargaon during 1904–09. He used to call Baba a mad fakir. When he came to Shirdi, Baba presented him with saffron clothes of a sanyasi. Bhate was then thoroughly transformed. He renounced mundane life and lived as a sanyasi in Shirdi. A devotee named Shri Sapathekar had lost his son. Baba brought him back in the form of their next child. Balakram Mankar renounced household life after the loss of his wife. Baba sent him to Machindragad for penance. There Baba appeared to Balakram to convince him that he was not contained to his 5½ foot body. Tatyasheb Noolkar came to Shirdi with Chandorkar. Baba granted him liberation at the time of leaving his mortal coil. Noolkar died at the holy feet of Baba in Shirdi. Sagun Meru Naik was a Datta devotee. Tembe Swami told Naik that he belonged to Shirdi darbar of Sai Baba. He left his residence and came to Shirdi. Baba made him open an inn at Shirdi and feed sadhus and fakirs. Anna Chinchanikar was a loving devotee. When plague broke out in Chinchani, Baba saved Mrs Chinchanikar, whose entire family was at Shirdi at that time. Chinchanikar donated his land to Shirdi sansthan. Just as Kaka Mahajani was taught Bhagwat by Baba, B.V. Deo of Kalyan was made to study Dhyaneshwari. He was also trained in asanas by Baba through visions. Nana Nimonkar was honorary Magistrate. He became united with the divine in Baba's company at Shirdi. He experienced eternal bliss while reciting Baba's name. Bapusaheb Jog came to Shirdi after retirement from service. There he spent his life performing Sai Baba's puja, arti and distributing the prasad. Khaparde sat in mute modesty in Baba's presence. He wrote *Khaparde Diary* which gives a realistic reflection of Baba's day-to-day routine, visitors and darbar in the Dwarkamai.

Dabholkar's *Sai Satcharitra* kept record of Sai Baba's life experiences and events. Baba prevailed upon his argumentative nature and turned him into a dedicated bhakta. His study of saint literature and love made the *Satcharitra* an authentic record, although it is not in strict chronology. This book is being read as a sacred pothi for the last four decades. Many devotees have been attracted to Sai through this book. The present book is a modification of earlier works. It aims at updating and extending Dabholkar's work. We have tried to make this biography more accommodative, chronological and pointed to bring forth the Guru aspect and eternal glory of the incarnation for the better understanding of a present-day reader. The mission of Baba for the welfare of mankind and uplift of humanity has been presented in proper perspective to enlighten modern devotee world. It has a universal approach.

Baba Decides to Cast Off His Mortal Coil

As we know, Baba's sojourn in Shirdi lasted from 1858 to 1918. Sixty years is a very long period for recognition of a saint with omnipotent powers and yogic siddhis such as his. An ordinary man retires at this stage! It was Nana and Ganu who spread Baba's glory to distant areas by their efforts. In 1904 and subsequent period, devotees like Sathe, Radhakrishna, Dixit, Bhishma,

Kushabhau, Upasani Maharaj carried his Guru mahima to religious people all over India and world. The illumination of Baba's Guruhood was recognized in 1909 and people came from distant places and thronged around Baba. Shirdi became a place of pilgrimage for all types of devotees, whether needy, desirous of earning fortune, indisposed or the higher type of bhaktas pining for atmic uplift. However, these last years from 1909 to 1918 were of Baba's ripe old age, when he was physically weak due to wear and tear of mundane existence. Baba therefore decided to cast off his physical encasement. Baba desired to cross the Makar constellation and turn left towards Hercules constellation in Sagittarius sign beyond which the bosom of the universe is operating as cosmic nucleus. The saints and sages of higher realized strata merge in the symbolic moon—a spiritual centre of cosmic awareness. Baba gave signs to his Sufi comrades and aulias that Allah would soon extinguish his lamp and he would thereafter operate on universal level of higher consciousness.

The Flame Finally Merges in Moon

Baba gave a vision to Bapusaheb Buti and Shyama simultaneously to build the temple of Muralidhar in the space flanked by the Gurusthan and the Dwarkamai. The work started in 1917, when Baba himself broke the coconut as an auspicious sign. Baba told them that he would stay in the wada (abode) after it was built and play with his children. This plot of land was full of big trees and presented dense forest-like appearance. Thorny plants and cactus growth was found in abundance. Insects, reptiles and scorpions used to stay within the bushes and thickets and Buti had to clear this all to make it worthy of habitation. To simple-minded Bapusaheb and Shyama it seemed Baba wanted Gopal Krishna Mandir to be built there. They never dreamt that he would transform the temple into his samadhi place. They supervised the construction of inner underground cell and the main hall. When the pedestal (on which the idol of Muralidhar Krishna was to be installed) was constructed, Baba told that he will come there to talk with his young comrades and associates. He told Uddhav Buva that he should not come to Shirdi hereafter. All these suggestions were specific and were pointers to Baba's impending samadhi. The flame of the Master was eager to finally merge in the lunar orb which denotes the symbolic crescent moon and the star of universal awareness as per spiritual parlance. This is the origin and final abode of saints, Masters and apostles.

Shamasuddin Miya Fakir and Fakir Banne Miya

These two Muslim Sufi cult aulias were bosom friends of Baba. They shared spiritual contact and rapport with Baba's soul. They were well versed in Sufi occultism and charismatic modes. It is true that Baba convinced Hindu devotees that he was Rama, Krishna, Shiva, Hanuman. But he was at the same time a product of Sufi Guru's grace and Sufi–Kabir cult sadhana. He never forgot Roshan Shah Fakir who was his fatherly guardian and Guru. His Sufi Guru uplifted him through his love and affection and his occult ways of granting sakshatkar (the realization experience). The Sufi way of grace transforms a disciple by mere touch or a token act of offering a tasted fruit. Divine awareness came as a Guru's gift to a disciple who became unconscious for days and after coming to senses found that he was fully realized and attuned to Allah. The memory and touch of his Guru had tinged Baba's whole life and he felt constantly indebted to the former. As Baba used to be surrounded by men of Hindu faith constantly in the masjid, his Muslim alienation was completely forgotten or thrown in the background. However, Baba was always in contact with his Sufi Master while he lived in the Dwarkamai. He said no one can be greater than Allah: 'Allah bhala karega.' The fakir in the mosque (he was called Datta also) was his guiding star in his day-to-day life, talks and teachings. References to aulias or fakirs of Aurangabad such as Shamasuddin and Banne Miya came to be explicit when Baba desired to take samadhi. It is to be observed with a keen eye and properly interpreted in the Muslim aulia tradition, how Baba sent his parting messages to these occult and eccentric-behavioured saints of Islam faith, as if they were a part and parcel of his spiritual self and had to work hereafter with the occult galaxy for the general welfare of humanity. Baba called Kasim, son of Bade Baba, and gave him some rotis and cooked chicken. Baba also gave him a sum of Rs 250 for handing it over to Shamasuddin. He asked Kasim and Chhote Khan to ask Shamasuddin to perform qawali, maulu and nyasa, which were the functions Muslims have to perform when a great soul departs. These are done to pave the soul's further passage to heaven. Thereafter Baba sent another Rs 250 with Kasim, Chhote Khan and Amir to Banne Miya, who was a far-advanced Muslim faith saint of occult actions and words. He was surrounded by a number of visitors and followers waiting to see him come out of his trance. The trio also had to wait.

Shamasuddin had known Baba's message and he had come himself to meet his guests. He uttered the actual words of the message to convince them of his identity. Banne Miya was in trance, but when the samadhi abated, he also uttered the exact message from Baba—'Nav Din, Nav Tarikh, Allah Apna Diya Bujhayega'! The trio was wonderstruck by the precognition of Banne Miya. As he gazed at the sky, tears streamed down his cheeks. Later he fed a large number of men and women with the sum of money sent by Sai Baba. Baba took the decision to leave his body quite early in 1916–17. The Vijaya Dashmi (Dussehra) date was prefixed. The events leading to his samadhi started unfolding when Ramchandra Patil fell ill in early 1918 and was on deathbed. Baba assured him that he would not die; instead Tatya Kote would fall ill and die on the Dussehra day.

Guru's Brick Breaks

In October 1918, Mahadu Fasle was as usual cleaning the mosque when the brick, which Baba's Guru Venkusha had given to him, fell down and broke into pieces. Baba was fully trained in Hindu shastras, dhyana, bhakti, karma, yoga by Venkusha, who was an example of Geeta–Bhagwat cult. Baba was an intelligent disciple. Destiny had arranged his coaching in Sufi–Kabir teachings as also in Hindu yoga bhakti cult to make him a perfect Master. The Hindu disciples of Venkusha were jealous and envied his love for a Muslim fakir boy and they tried to hurt Baba. One threw a brick on his head and wounded him, but Venkusha saved him. As Venkusha was to take samadhi in a few days, he ordered Baba to leave his ashram and to meet Swami Samartha, the great Datta cult incarnation. Before leaving his ashram, Venkusha blessed Baba, milked a dry cow which was passing by in a lamana (gipsy) group and extracted three seers of milk. He made Baba drink these three (symbolical) seers of dhyana, bhakti and yoga. He encased Baba's karma in the brick that had hurt him and asked him to carry on his mission with blessings from the Datta incarnation. Baba left the ashram in 1854. When the brick broke that day, Baba took it as a signal for departure. He said, 'Karma encasement has broken.' The brick was his life partner. He had to leave his mortal coil. *Sai Geetayan* says, 'The confinement of karma ended. The Master has to leave and assume cosmic dimensions.' Baba had already decided to leave. This was the final sign. He gave vision to Das Ganu at Pandharpur that he was leaving Shirdi because the grocers and oil extractors had pestered him enough. He also told Purandare and Dixit that he was leaving and that they had to follow his steps. His turbat will speak, bless and play with the devotees. The exit was predestined.

Three Palanquins Wait at the Village Outskirts

Baba had told an ailing Ramchandra Patil that three carriers were waiting at Shirdi's boundary but he would not allow the former to be taken away. He will send them back. But Tatya's destiny was to be sealed on Dussehra day. Gradually, Tatya Kote fell ill and his health deteriorated day-by-day. Baba sent him some udi. At the same time, Baba himself contracted fever and became weak. He ordered Tatya to be brought over to him. He blessed Tatya and slowly the latter's health started improving. Baba accepted his sickness and was determined to go in place of Tatya. Baba had sent Ramachandra's carrier back. Remaining two carriers were for Baba and Tatya. Baba sent back the second one also, which was for Tatya, and reserved the third for himself. He asked the devotees to read *Hari Vijaya* in the mosque. He heard it three times before his mahasamadhi. Three days prior to Vijaya Dashmi, Baba told his devotees that he would cross the boundaries (simollanghan) on the said day. This meant that he would end his physical life on 15 October 1918 and so it happened. Baba called Laxmibai Shinde (who used to feed him with bread and onion) and told her that his body had been fostered on her food and as such he was indebted to her. He gave nine silver coins symbolising nine-fold (nava-vidhi) bhakti to her. After the arti was finished on the Dussehra day of 1918, Baba sent all bhaktas home to take their food. Only Bayaji, Laxmi, Bhagoji, Kashiram Shimpi and Nana Nimonkar were present in the Dwarkamai when Baba departed to his divine abode. Baba told them that he was not feeling well and wished to be taken to Buti Wada (Murlidhar temple). Baba cast his body leaning his head on the shoulder of Bayaji. Nimonkar put Ganga water in his mouth as the last ritual to a dying man. The mundane life of Sai Baba ended here. The entire Shirdi and bhakti world was flooded by grief. Balasaheb Bhate and Upasani Maharaj performed the final rites of Baba. The two personalities are very little mentioned in *Sai Satcharitra*. Hence ordinary pothi bhaktas have only meagre information about them. Such are the glaring gaps in the authentic *Charitra*.

Hindu–Muslim Dispute on Final Rites

As in the case of Kabir, who was Baba's previous incarnation, Hindus and Muslims were in difference about the nature of Baba's final rites. The mamlatdar of Kopargaon was fortunately present on the spot, who settled the matter and Baba rested on the Murlidhar platform of Buti Mandir. Baba desired to play from this auspicious place with bhaktas after his demise. It happened so. *Sai Geetayan* says:

> 'The Bansidhar Sai has come to repose in Murlidhar Temple.
> The chetana emancipated from body is open to play in Cosmic Temple of Divine.
> Although the body of clay has bonds, the soul has no boundaries.
> The tomb still moves with words of love and prayer.
> The pranas throb in the earth and the super soul works out wonders.
> The soul reacts, responds to devotees.
> The bones themself become live and speak to us with compassion.'

27

Baba Crosses Mundane Borders

When a human being ends his life, we say that he has expired or he is no more. We also term it as if he has been summoned by God or he has departed to Vaikuntha or Kailash according to his faith. When a great social or national figure is no more, we call it as a mahayatra, mahaprayan, or mahanirvana. In the case of a sadhu, we say he has merged in God or taken mahasamadhi. However, Saint Dhyaneshwar's own voluntary samadhi is called 'sanjeevan samadhi', for he chose to remain in constant state of super conscious or divine awareness. Sai Baba's samadhi is known as his entrance into higher Mahakarna body or super conscious existence. It is really the assimilation state by which he crossed the borders of limited human body to remain ever-alive, perpetually working for the welfare of humanity from a very higher Satchitananda level of eternal Guruhood.

The great divine mahatmas have no beginning or end. This is because their transphysical self reigns supreme over time, space, five elements as a perpetual *chaitanya* (sentience). They do not sprout from birth. They do not perish with death. Their incarnating self takes new forms or bodies for their mission of uplift and welfare of humanity. Their life, work and teachings constitute their real existence. Baba was a constant, unending, ever-alive divine incarnation. Baba's mahasamadhi was not extinction, it was the transformation of the divinity into a colossal universal super consciousness level. It was ever-sentient sanjeevan state or a cosmic assimilation where he works with God's omnipotent power.

Yoga Samadhi

Men of meagre understanding are tempted to compare Baba's departure form physical world as a yogi's samadhi. This is an ignorance of his avataric nature and amounts to limiting his divinity. We would not try such unintelligent comparisons here at all. Patanjal yoga (the secret knowledge) explains the samadhi state of a yogi which is a merger into nothingness of the entire desires, passions, designs, sentiments, mind, vital airs, intellect and ego. All impulses, attachments and controls are to be fully obliterated. The creative power of causal body is also to be dissolved. The awareness which comes into contact with avidya and makes sankalpas must also be fully wiped out. The entire being is merged into sentience at the time of deluge. Similarly, all in mayic world must merge in atmic state. Unless the sound and light in savikalpa also melts, samadhi state cannot be achieved. The non-duality must be fully reached by merging into everformless, steady Kaivalya pada (state). Then only final nirvana which is called Kaivalya mukti can be achieved by yogi. The state of avataric mahatmas is beyond this normal state of mukta yogis. We cannot compare Siddha avatars with normal yogis who endeavour for their own realization or liberation.

The Unparalleled Glory of Avataric Siddhas

The great Avadhoota Siddhas appear on earth to uplift and enlighten humanity. There are both Muslim and Hindu siddhas who fall in this category. Some of them are Tajuddin Baba, Sai Baba, Moinuddin, Khwaja (Gareeb-Nawaj), Haji Malang, Nityananda, Gajanan Maharaj, Shankar Maharaj, Swami Samarth, etc. The saintly Avadhootas of this category live a life unbound by rules and regulations. They perform multitude of miracles to assist their loyal and surrendered followers. Their life, teaching and exposition is clouded in mystery and occultism and hence men of reason who are educated and elite do not pay attention to them or deride their greatness in sheer ignorance. This is why their lives have not been properly studied, appreciated and their philosophy and mission correctly understood in proper perspective. Bhagwat saints like Dhyaneshwar and Tukaram, (although they were put to trials and humiliations at initial stages) have been studied and understood in past 500 to 700 years. The Siddhas however have been underrated and derided upon because of lack of study and understanding of their life, purpose and mission. People approach them for redress of their difficulties, ailments, destitution but then soon forget them, their philosophy and message after selfish interests are fulfilled. Elite and educated rationalists look at Siddhas with suspicion because their behaviour and mannerism is unconventional and above normal codes. The mechanical arguments that siddhis deter spiritual progress also come in the way of their appreciation and understanding. In order to adjudge and estimate the work done by Siddhas in the field of human uplift and welfare, a genius is required to be born to educate ordinary people about the ground position. The ignorance and short memory are the faults in society. The hard penance and self-control do earn powers for the Siddhas. Their hearts are full of pity and compassion and limitless like the expanse of sky. Swami Samarth, Sai Baba and other philanthropic, humanitarian saints of stupendous powers and mercy have not been properly studied in the context of their life, mission and purpose. Their miracles are either extolled or belittled by people, who mislead intellectual and educated layers of society. The philosophy and sadhana of Nath, Datta, Kabir, Sufi saints is occult and challenges intellect and creative acumen of learned authors as well as historians. Commenting on Saint Dhyaneshwar's ovi stanzas and Tukaram's abhangas is easier and commands respect, whether the commentator and his reader knows the real substance or not. Interpretation of life and words of occult saints like Sai Baba and Swami Samarth is difficult and many are not therefore inclined to touch the area. Their secret knowledge surpasses human logic and reason. Shraddha can understand them.

Baba's Simollanghan (Crossing of Border)

After eighty-three years of physical existence in this world, Baba decided to wound his leelas and work on a new cosmic plane. His Satchitananda Guru form was eternal in its true nature and substance. The common man was incapable of fathoming this knowledge and could only be known by experience of higher spiritual type. This was not a sunset, a demise or even a mahanirvana. It was sanjeevan state of being in the terms of Dhyaneshwari in atmic parlance. Common people moaned that Baba had departed. But it was a misconception as Baba did not die. He conquered physical death, for the Guru incarnation cannot end and be bound by birth and death. Baba had crossed the borders of the quarters, time and space. His hand of succour comes down with compassion and love to help us even today. The heart still throbs out of the grave and the hand still touches our forehead in blessings and consoles our ailing, agonised hearts.

The Vision to Shyama Ganu

On the next day of his samadhi, Baba appeared to Shyama and said, 'Shyama, Bapusaheb will not turn up to masjid for my daily puja because he thinks that I am dead. The ignorant souls have not yet known that I am eternal super soul, cosmic divinity. You come with Laxman mama and perform my ritual puja as before.' Das Ganu was at Pandharpur then. He had a vision that Baba manifested before him and said, 'Ganu, I am leaving Shirdi. The grocers and the oil extractors have pestered me enough. I want to leave. Come, Ganu, and decorate my body with flowers.' Baba's state was ever alive, ever sentient. The sanjeevan or samarasya state of assimilation in cosmic soul made him omniscient, omnipresent and omnipotent in a more powerful way than when he was encased in human body.

A New View of Sai Baba's Avatarhood

Dhyaneshwar, the great Bhagwat saint from Maharashtra, had at the end of his spiritual treatise on Geeta invoked the cosmic Gurudev in his famous prayer named 'Pasayadan'.

> 'O cosmic Guru principle, grant me the boon that the darkness of the evil may vanish and the world adhere to the solar orb of swadharma (righteous duties). The wicked would cast their crookedness. Duality would end. Unity would rule the world society.'

He knew that this type of change cannot happen with the merits of a single saint or sadhu. Men of religious faith and unity with God must come together to form a positive and dynamic cluster at every small and big place. For this, a new incarnation of cosmic Guru or God was a necessity. God himself must incarnate and lead small groups of upright and righteous men to establish dharma. Geeta promises through the words of Lord Krishna that God incarnates in ages for the establishment of dharma, annihilation of the wicked and the evildoers and for the help and uplift of pious men and women. Universal God through incarnation of Sai Baba, Swami Samarth and such great epoch-maker incarnations answered this prayer of Dhyaneshwar.

He Came with Father's Love and Mother's Compassion

Yet Baba had a greater characteristic. His love and compassion crossed the borders of sects, castes and religions. It embraced entire humanity. Baba's supreme soul crossed all limits and discriminations to uphold the welfare of the humanity and uplift of the mankind. In brief, he was universal Guruhood.

Guru Incarnation of Love and Compassion Leads Humanity towards Peace and Liberation

We do not want to end the story with Baba's mahasamadhi for Baba's avatar has no end. Let us pause a bit in 1918 and take note of the divine rebirth of Guruhood in enormous proportions and limitless directions. The mission of the Guru has carried on unendingly till this hour. We have also not delineated individuals appearing after 1918 with the events and experiences in their lifetime in association with Baba. There are countless small and big personalities with higher experiences and vision of Baba's grace since then. The lives of Rege, Tarkhad, Pradhan, Galwankar, Purandare, Narke and Muslim devotees who came in contact with Baba in his mortal form have found sufficient light in the present available biographies by Dabholkar, Narasimha Swami and others. A separate story will have to be written to enumerate experiences of all who followed Baba after 1918. Here we end this biography with portrayal of Baba as an epoch-making but benign Guru incarnation.

Epoch-Making but Simple Life

Sai Baba was an epoch-making Guru incarnation of the present age. He not only raised the banner of universal love but also illumined the religious horizon of India and the world with divine grace. Apart from toughness of Vedic religion, Baba is the rigid devotion of Vaishnavas. His exposition and direction is unique beyond all barriers of religion, castes, sects, creeds and cults. He blends in himself all religious cults including dhyana, yoga, bhakti as well as Sufi, Kabir, Nath and Datta sadhanas.

Beyond Parameters of Learned

Sai Baba, though outwardly simple and benign, is beyond the grasp of symbolic tests and criteria prescribed by scholars. He cannot be fettered in the parameters and adjudged. He has not written books, voluminous religious texts or given abstract sermons. He cannot be fixed in the frame with saints Dhyaneshwar and Eknath. He cannot be recognized as an originator of a new religion. He cannot be included among Siddhas doing penance in high mountain ranges away from the mundane life to escape from the agony and torture of human existence. He is not even classed among householder saints like Chidambar Dixit who upheld the lifestyle of karma path prescribed by shastras and religious lore. He is a potent Avadhoota of the stature of Swami Samarth of Akkalkot. He resembles eccentric and self-willed mahatmas, who were unpredictable in words and deeds. He always remained within limit of decency and high morality. He had some queer characteristics and strange behaviour but he cannot be detached from the society. His way of talking, uplifting and edifying, doing miracles was to some extent comparable to Siddhas like Tajuddin, Haji Malang of the Vali or aulia cult. His mammoth accomplishment of humanitarian work and unification of the disunited Indian society would make him unique and unparalleled in as much as he cannot be compared with any earlier mahatma. Even Kabir, who is said to be his earlier incarnation, was limited in scope and achievement, if examined in juxtaposition with Sai Baba.

Thus Sai Baba has a significant and independent place in the religious and spiritual history of India. He was uplifting, compassionate, unworldly but a unifying source of grace at once humane in approach and balanced in equality and equanimity. This unequalled position of an epoch-making incarnation is unique. He is not merely a common saint or not even a doyen among the saints. His omnipotence, omniscience and omnipresence as also his existence from times immemorial indicated that Baba was the divine power of Guru which is all pervading, immortal and merged in the universal consciousness or the cosmic mind as yogis describe. He has been appearing in every age to help the suffering humanity, steeped in the mirage of sansara. This was an antidote to the poison of modern times.

Employment of Miracles

Another unique feature of Baba's personality was his indulgence in the divine miracles in order to save, edify or salvage his devotees. Generally miracle-mongering by men of spiritual power is criticized and prohibited by men of sagacity, discrimination and wisdom as they are supposed to be deterrent and harmful to the spiritual aspirants. But here Baba was an exception to the common rule. Miracles were performed by him to the maximum extent in a most liberal or munificent manner. Baba's existence was itself a miracle, as the omnipotent power of the universe was personified in his frail fakir frame. Baba cannot be separated from his wonderful powers to perform great miracles. We love Baba for his miracles and cannot conceive him apart from his miraculous divinity. His miracles were the most natural exposition or manifestation of his incarnation. They showed that the God has indeed come on the earth. He was unbound by time, space and causation. The past, the present and the future were an open book to him. The sanchita and prarabdha karmas were nullified at his very will. Baba's volition was accepted by the nature as a command and the whole atmosphere adjusted to it.

Even being fully conscious of his mahima, Baba appeared, acted and spoke like a common man in the forlorn Shirdi hamlet. He loved the pious ones and reprimanded the wicked. He instilled faith in the minds of those who loved God.

Operation of Grace

We have seen above how the perfect Master of Baba's stature could react with a bhakta to present a glimpse of his all-pervading omniscient divinity in the modern age full of stresses, tensions, trials and tribulations, light and shade, weal and woe, agony and pleasure. These are the products of modern times and Baba catered to the requirements of devotees to harmonise with the pace of time.

But what is the essence of Baba's Gurupath? We would say that it is not mere nama as in Kabir incarnation. The oral teachings of the Sai incarnation bordered around Guru bhakti and Guru dhyana of the Nath or Datta cult. Constant fixing of one's mind on the form of Guru leads to instant link with the Guru principle. Baba has himself said that the Guru lights the flame of realization. Guru protects the disciple just as a female tortoise protects her babies from a distance and leads the disciple to their goal. The walls between both do fall and collapse. Sai enters the disciple's body (both physical and subtle, maybe even causal). This is his mahakripa. This is because the supreme grace takes disciple's karmas as naishkarmas, sentiments rise to bhav-avastha, dhyana is raised to sahaj-avastha. The mind is then lifted automatically to the turiya stage. Jiva is transformed into Shiva when unmana stage rises as a final stage of enlightenment. The super conscious self is slowly led to cosmic consciousness or universal awareness. This is called samarasya, a stage even higher than the samadhi stage. The disciple stands on equal throne with God, and japa, tapa, mantra then become unnecessary. Intense devotion, balanced discrimination, surrendered karma and merger of yoga become a natural and common disposition. This is real discipleship which is rare in all ages, whether bygone, modern or future. Baba was Guru, his mission was diffusion of grace.

Reaction to Those Who Approached Him

Whenever a bhakta approached Baba, he strengthened the former's faith in his original deity by a suitable vision. To seekers of moksha, Baba preached discrimination, dhyana, service, equity, equanimity and humane attitude. He asked men and women to recite 'Rajaram' or 'Sai' as the name of Rama flowed through his blood since his Kabir manifestation. Baba told ordinary men and women to recite any name dear to them because all names of godheads were his own names and all merged in Sai nama. He prescribed that love was the primary basis of bhakti and steady bhava sustained and nurtured grace. He declared that those bhaktas who were loyal to him and did not act, think or eat without remembering him were dearer to him than his own soul. He would offer his own life to save them. He told all those nearer to him that he was not God. He was their father. Baija, Shyama and Mhalsapathi were given intimate direction by the Shirdi Gurushakti. From more evolved persons he begged for the alms of their mind, body, intellect and ego, so that he could take possession of their life and lead and guide them as the eternal charioteer, just as Lord Krishna guided Arjuna.

Chandorkar and Ganu were asked to perform their day-to-day duties in dedication to Sai or God. Immersion of body, mind, consciousness and ego in God and his love was a virtual mukti for those devoted and dedicated to him. He would then enter into the bhakta's life and lead him to light eliminating his burdens and salvaging his life from the bonds of karma. To higher bhaktas he explained how ego entangled karma in chains, and how a human being falls prey to the prarabdha, creating new karma and sanchita for new birth only because he cannot cast his ego and abandon fruits of karmas.

To Mhalsapathi, pious, virtuous life of puja and bhakti and non-attachment to money or luxury was adequate, but to Dengle and Chandorkar what was important was the above dhyana type of preaching especially prescribed by Sai Baba. Pure devotion was sufficient for the simpleton Megha but for Upasani, higher tenets of yoga burning his jiva dasha by physical and mental sufferings (enjoining the vision of universal merger and lustre of spiritual sun), was an essential mode of training imparted by Baba. Ganu was floated on the waves by sentiment of devotion and service to saints in the form of poetry, kirtan and propaganda. Commotion was aroused by Baba in Das Ganu so that he could flood the society in gushes of devotion. Baba's versatile spiritual personality was meeting the varying needs of his devotees according to their capacities and yearnings.

Simple Teaching for the Modern Age

Here we would like to reiterate and emphasize the simpler aspects of Baba's teaching for a modern age average man. Baba said, 'Allah is the Master. None other is greater than God. God again is the single Master of the universe, world itself is his own manifestation. God is beyond all religions and is not shackled by caste, creed, religion and other discriminations. He is chaitanya and chaitanya only. He leads to uplift and liberate the soul. This raises the consciousness to higher height. Hence he is the universal Guru uplifting the humanity, purifying it with his divine love and ambrosial compassion. He does not live in mosques but the entire world is his temple. Human heart is for reciting his name, form, glory. No peace would be forthcoming without forsaking sinful and narrow desires and evil acts. God is most powerful and relieving when you treat him as Guru. God comes in the form of cosmic Guru to emancipate, uplift and infuse mankind with knowledge, discrimination, love and sadhana.

Guru Is Baba's Ultimate Form

Guruhood is the essence Sai story. Hence Baba's charitra is verily Guru charitra. This has no beginning, nor end. The Gurus never take birth or die. Hence Baba's life is perpetual, Guru Geeta or the saga of Guru incarnation. The story creates equality, unity and supreme awareness and flows through centuries of human existence. We shall not therefore end this biography with a note of samadhi event. We hold that Baba was reborn as great and universal Guru in 1909, assumed cosmic form in 1918 and continued his universal mission without a break or interception. Baba's work expanded, enlarged, multiplied and flew in manifold torrents, covered all the nooks and corners of India and the entire world. Baba broke the walls of human gradations, differences of caste, creed, sects and brought humanity on the common platform of equality, brotherhood and amity. He invoked the inner soul of every individual, improved human thinking and deeds, changed destiny (prarabdha, kriyamana and sanchita) under the umbrella of his compassion and opened all doors for liberation of human soul. This was a great alchemy. Baba's love was so intense, seething and liberating that all narrow thought and actions were getting purified in the Ganges water springing up from his Himalayan heart. The single religion of love, the singular Satchitananda principle and the mission of uniting the world was identified with this great Guru avatar. Let us abandon our petty and contaminated thoughts and face the incarnation with wholehearted surrender for the uplift and welfare of our souls. Baba used his siddhis to lend a hand of succour to the needy, ailing and destitute. Sai Baba did not turn away even those who approached him for paltry gains. His miracles joined a golden border of shraddha and saburi to the selfish, self-centred folk. He lent metaphysical touch to the householders. When the men stood astounded at his wish-fulfilling tree, they became dhyani and Mumukshu learning faith and perseverance. Baba uplifted the common folk without wordy lectures or sermons, by his direct method, action and experience. Baba, in fact, touched the modern age and changed its texture.

Beyond the Mundane Limits

Baba was the divine power moving on the dusty pathways of the physical world. The sky seemed to touch the earth. The human element was embracing heavenly divinity in his frail-looking frame. Baba's life was inwardly a paradox. Nobody knew about his home, but the entire world was his house. All names were his own names. He used to sit at one place and move the entire universe. His dwelling in the mosque transformed it into a mandir. He sat before the dhuni. The confluence of Hindu, Muslim, Parsi culture was present in his lifestyle and breeding. He was a blend of Sufi, Nath, Datta cult sadhanas of Guru bhakti, yoga and devotion.

His speech and deeds resembled his earlier incarnation of Kabir. He used to beg for alms but the goddess of wealth, Lakshmi, was his maidservant. He used to fly with rage but preached peace and self-control to us. He accepted dakshina but retained not a single pie for his own use. He did not deliver lectures or sermons but the entire Vedanta exuded from his acts and talks. He was a renunciate but he was full of compassion and love for the humanity. He was not a householder but he bore the burden of the welfare, sustenance and subsistence of his householder followers. He had no religion, caste or creed to profess but he was a champion and votary of humanity and service to human beings. He offered his life for saving a devotee's life. This divine and strange paradox was the mystery of his existence. There had been many saints, dhyanis, yogis and siddhas in Maharashtra before Sai Baba. There have also been thinkers, spiritualists, authors, poets among saintly persons like Dhyaneshwar, Namdev, Eknath, Tukaram etc. The soil of this land is wet because of the showers of Geeta and Bhagwat philosophy for seven long centuries. Yet Sai Baba shines apart from them with his simple, plain life, speech and style of manifestation and teachings. He created Dabholkars, Das Ganus, Mhalsapathis in large number from all sections of society, whether illiterate, learned, elite or high placed. His shraddha and saburi demanded faith, surrender, dedication and tenacity to face the odds of life in utter allegiance to God.

It is now known to inquisitive and research-minded devotees that Baba was associated with Sufi cult through his guardian father Roshan Shah Fakir who had initiated him in Quran, Muslim type of sadhana, Sufi-disciple relationship and the mystery of Allah's grace. This was akin to Natha and Datta cult Guru–shishya relation. Eradication of ego and surrender to Guru was a direct heritage of the Sufi tenet of Roshan Shah Fakir. Baba referred to this fatherly Guru in his life very often and narrated this in his symbolic metaphorical anecdotes or stories.

His next Guru was Venkusha or Gopal Swami who was a Bhagwat saint and an administrator in Nizam Kingdom. It is pointed out by avatar Shri Meher Baba that Baba came in contact with Swami Samarth of Akkalkot as well during his travelling spell of 1854 to 1858. Baba used to be in ecstasy and was hurled in his lifelong natural state of sahaj samadhi by the Swami. This makes us to infer that the Master's touch put his divinity in duel consciousness of operating on physical and metaphysical super consciousness and cosmic level, for Swami was a direct Dattavatar (dynamo of power). Thus Baba's breeding of his own personality was faceted by all aspects—devotional, Siddha-yogic, Bhagwat, aulia or Vali, fakir. His perfect status made him accessible to all those who approached him, whether high or low, affluent or destitute, materialistic or spiritual. In short, Baba's spiritual upbringing was a confluence of various cults, which made him a many-faceted Master to cater to the needs of new age. He was a perfect Master, perfect Guru avatar.

This is eventually the end of Sai story. The Guru incarnation is perpetual, unending and ever present in its omniscient, omnipotent form. We promise to illumine further facets of Sai glory in a separate volume in near future.

Epilogue

We present in a unique way Sai Baba's alchemy to uplift, edify, reform and liberate not only man but entire mankind in the next section, captioned 'Sai Baba and Sadhana'.

Appendix

Sai Baba and Sadhana
(A Rediscovery of Sai Way to Salvation)

We are aware that speaking about sadhana in relation to Sai Baba is an uncommon and unthinkable topic. This is because a common devotee approaches Sai Baba mainly for material benefits. He is unable to apprehend the noble purpose for which the incarnation of Sai appeared on this earth. Even learned devotees have not understood the great multilateral inner reform, which Sai avatar intends to bring out in the mankind. The reason is that Baba never gave any mantra–tantra sadhana. His upadesh or message is not couched in words or books. He brings direct change of heart, raising human body to purity and piety, human mind to virtue and intense love for Guru, human intellect to the super conscious level of higher cosmic awareness leading the human existence to Satyam, Shivam and Sundaram which is the perfection, the ideal of Indian culture, lifting humanity to liberation, unity, uniformity and atmic realized state. Thus the purpose of Sai Baba's life and mission stands misunderstood by both rustics as well as elites, young and old, ignorant and prudent men and women. These sequences try to lift this curtain of adhyana and reveal Sai path.

Common Man's Approach

Whenever a common man meets a saint, his purpose is to secure material benefits or worldly gains through his divine power. There is very little understanding in men and women that the purpose of life is to the reach the abode of ananda by adopting proper lifestyle, both mental and intellectual attitude and to uplift human awareness to higher level of divine consciousness. This is sadhana way of life. A life without spiritual sadhana is directionless and betrays the very aim for which we have taken birth on this earth. The lust or lure of power, fame, luxury, wealth and indulgence in physical pleasure is mayic and fleeting and deprives a human being of his legitimate right to establish himself in love, peace and divine contentment.

Reaction of Saints and Seers to This Attitude

Two great saints in Maharashtra, namely Sai Baba of Shirdi and Gondavalekar Maharaj of Shri Ram Nam sect from Gondavale used to regret for the common attitude of devotees who approached them and thronged around them for their motives behind satsang. The intention was mainly to resolve day-to-day difficulties and sansarik oddities. Nobody had the real intention to undertake sadhana or lead a life of atmic peace or spiritual realization. Sai Baba declared to these devotees that he was much disappointed to see that none of them had come to accept the wealth which Baba's Guru wanted to donate to his followers. We can realize that only very limited men and women led a spiritual life of virtue, piety and sadhana discipline. Among Baba's own devotees, none was his disciple. Only few reached atmic height and that also with Baba's own munificent grace and compassion. They must understand that God does not want your flowers, fruits and shawls. He wants pure, dedicated heart and faithful sadhana connection. What people give is not their own. It is what God himself has owned and created. The pure mind, faith and dedication of heart are devotees' own valued gift, which they do not offer or surrender to God or Guru!

Sai Baba's Advice to Common Devotee

Baba told his devotees that many times he fulfils the wishes of his followers because they learn the value of faith and then listen to his advice. They are then ready to receive with open minds whatever higher wealth Baba offers them for their ultimate good. The grant of favours is not for demanding more and more worldly gains. It is to imbibe shraddha and saburi. He desires to show them that he is their indweller. He is not a prisoner in the cage of body. He is timeless, space-less, omnipresent, omnipotent Guru or God. He is latent in their vital breath. They had to shower their mind, buddhi, body and soul on the indweller Baba. Pure love, service without expectation, self-knowledge and constant contemplation was his puja and worship. Desire this wealth now only because Baba would not be available so easily after the rainy season of his showering grace recedes or subsides. Thus Baba's effort was to discourage common man from following cheap and orthodox ways of selfish and fruit-oriented devotion. It is not in reality devotion. It is a bargain, an exchange, a barter under high labels of devotion, religion or austerities!

Change of Life Direction

The main principle or basis for laying the foundation of Sai orientation is to first purify body, mind and soul to deserve grace and divine sympathy. God cannot alight on a dirty or unclean ground. The life of desire, benefit mongering, selfish motive must abate and we must rise up to love and serve humanity or world at large if we aspire to be Sai men. The centre of selfishness must be out of its circumference. It must be replaced or substituted by love for God, love for humanity. The present direction of common individual life strengthens man's lust for organic pleasures and accumulation of money as well as satisfaction of selfish interests with special stress of mind as 'I' and 'mine'. This does not allow purity of benign love and virtues but contracts its sphere towards selfishness. Baba wants to transform human life whirling around selfish aims and to redirect it to divine self.

Not Only Guru but Healthy Life Demands Change

Baba likes selfless and innocent mind. This is also a demand to improve present-day hypocrisy and imbibe godliness in life to become healthy. The dual behaviour and hypocrisy are detrimental to spiritual life and atmic progress. This invites corruption, violence and mental derangement. To improve society, we have to reform individually by making human mind selfless, seva-oriented, full of piety, human virtues and divine good qualities. This also lays foundation of spiritual and philanthropic values of godward progression of an individual reforming soul.

Selfish Interest and Division of Mind Conceals God

Divine virtues, purity of mind and intellect is the very base where sadhana can be sown and rich crop of virtuous life can be harvested. Men and women must lay this foundation to erect the edifice of divine life. When the mind is quiet, peaceful without ripples of lust and desire, the God principle automatically pervades empty recesses and reserves of human life. This is indeed self-realization because what is called self or atma is itself the love, truth or divinity—whatever you may like to call it. The truth shines itself with its divine real splendour, when the ripples of mind, desires and thoughts die down. The self is self-shining and self-manifesting. When the clouds of doubt, ignorance and false ideas vanish, the atmic sun sheds its golden rays in human consciousness.

Common Concept about Sadhana

Ordinary people are beset with wrong ideas about sadhana as also Sai Baba. Going to places of pilgrimage, reading texts and life stories of philosophers, karmic rigid rituals like yajna, tapas, baths and fasts, etc. are quoted as great sadhana ways. Recitation of mantras, living in caves and monasteries, leading a sanyasi's life are also supposed to be sadhana. Baba never certified such fasts, rituals or austerities. He preached and judged inner piety, uplifting and transformation. Hence he never encouraged mantra, tantra, daan, sacrifice etc. He knew that unless the mind and intellect are purified, no grace can descend, no experience be transcended into any sadhana. He himself was a model of sadhana, a Siddha. He was Satchitananda Satguru himself, fully evolved and capable of revolution by mere touch of sankalpa or grace. Some elite persons even described Baba gathering idle, lazy, rustic, good-for-nothing villagers and wasting his own as well as their valuable time. They rarely knew that Baba was Malanga Dattatreya himself. His silence was sermon, his words were upadesh and his single glance was grace.

Misunderstanding Baba's Guruhood

The misunderstanding of Sai Baba's role as a Guru had its origin in the fact that Baba's miracles made ignorant people see him as a miracle man. They recognized him as a demand-fulfiller avatar, without understanding his mission or purpose. Once their wishes were fulfilled, they disappeared from the scene and reappeared only when the next demand arose. There was no duty, no obligation and no obedience. Baba did not give Guru mantra to anybody, hence his alchemy reforming men of faith remained unseen and unrecognized. Baba's style of Sufi eccentricity and occult Guruhood could not be appreciated for a long time till he attracted Nana, Ganu, Megha, Mhalsapathi, Dengle. They were being transformed by Baba gradually during 1858 to 1909. But it was so slow and unnoticeable that common men could not comprehend this fundamental overhauling of body, mind and soul. Only when great men of faith and allegiance and great personalities immersed in Guru bhakti came to Shirdi after 1890, Baba's Guru status could slowly come to horizon and be understood.

Why Baba Did Not Manifest His True Potency

Baba had appeared on the horizon as an extension of Kabir birth. He came with true sadhana, unity of human beings, reconciliation of religions and mission for uplifting mankind which Kabir incarnation had left unfinished. But during his first fifty years, he developed his penance and helped ailing, destitute men and women in a limited manner befitting his stay and lifestyle in Shirdi village. In 1886, Allah did not approve his wish to withdraw from the world scene and merge in universal bliss. He sent him back to Shirdi to work out his unfinished karma of attracting humanity to the sublime goal of life of collective emancipation. He accepted the new role and slowly attracted learned and propagating men like Nana and Das Ganu to spread his mahima. He collected a large following in Shirdi by 1900, who adored him as an avatar. They established his throne in Shirdi as a world teacher and Satchitananda Satguru who aimed at emancipating the humanity reconciling all faiths and religions, uniting the world under one banner of cosmic Guru for uplifting the human race to its ultimate goal of realization.

Universal Guru Who Transforms Humanity

The role of universal Guru reforming the mind, intellect and lifestyle of humanity was accepted by Baba in 1909. He shines as Guru supreme. He gave no mantra or initiation. He saw into the karmas of men and women, tried to correct their contaminated souls by direct grace and endeavoured to join them to the path of perfection, leading themselves to the status of Satyam, Shivam and Sundaram. Baba knew that mere mantra cannot change a heart. There should be total purification and sublimation of individual at all levels (body, mind, buddhi, ego and atma). This change he could bring with the magic of his touch or alchemy of his divine grace. Big crowds of devotees thronged around Shirdi from 1910 to 1918 and Shirdi became a place of universal pilgrimage after Baba's mahasamadhi. However, the persons who approached him could intake his grace and transform themselves to the extent the faith, allegiance and sincerity they brought with them. The virtues, purity, piety, dedication and will to adapt according to Baba's dictates were the main criteria to receive Baba's grace. It was abundant to those who deserved.

Real Meaning of Sadhana

We have so far seen how the life and words of saints or seers are in themselves a model or example of direct teaching of sadhana. The lecturers or pandits cannot teach direct sadhana and actual experiencing. They can only interpret or comment on a saint's life and his words in their own way. Saints shape the life itself into liberation or moksha. They are themselves the live illustration of their own philosophy. We miss sadhana because we turn our back to benign, straightforward, innocent ways of behaviour and move away from service of others and unselfish love. We miss God because our ego misdirects us to self-centred, selfish activities, which take us in the reverse direction. Thus we fail to see the divine, although it is standing next to our self. In brief, Sai is the soul and Shirdi is the abode of emancipation and bliss.

Material Life Versus Divine Love

Baba has shown the existence of God in day-to-day life but we fail to understand this truth and cling to the readymade concepts prevailing in society. We think that lonely life in caves, meditation in deep forests, fasting, puja, dhyana, austerities mean sadhana. The real sadhana dwells not in these mechanical processes but in love, devotion, surrender and dedication in intense degree interwoven in these acts. Love without expectation, intense devotion, unceasing brooding over name and form is essential for a sadhaka's life. Thus all outward acts are futile and ineffective if mind is not pure, faith is not steady, intellect is not resolute and soul is not divine. If it is so and the emotions are intense, life itself will automatically turn into sadhana process. Saffron clothes, garland of beads, outward equipments of sanyasi's life, staying in ashram and disciple-infested monastery does not make one a sadhaka. We must rehabilitate ourselves in our benign, inborn innocence and purity which we gained at our very birth but later squandered in the heat of selfish and self-centred pursuits. The heart of mundane life has fettered us in 'I' and 'my' orientation and we have deviated from the presence and proximity of God. Competition, ambition, fear and jealousy have crippled our nobility and made our life frugal, restricted, envious and intolerant. The experiences of men and events unfavourable to our self-esteem and self-interest, the din and dust of heated existence have divested us from the ideal mental equilibrium leading to peace and amity.

Downfall of Man from Sadhana Path

An impaired mind, buddhi and ego cannot allow the life to flow with essential purity and piety, which leads to liberation and bliss. Company of saints and sadhana are the only saviours, which can rehabilitate the morbid mind to its original innocence and goodwill. In such condition of downfall, Baba used to help, cure and re-establish the human mind, improve the hypocritic and selfish turn of life and rejoin the devoted person to the right mentality and right path. He made the surrendered person concentrate on all his failings and leave him at the feet of the Lord and broaden his mental plane to receive divine intervention and God's grace.

Breaking of Bonds of Lust and Lure

Baba admonished that the lies of desire and passion should be dissolved and the mind, buddhi and ego be freed from the prison of mayic power. Then only can the soul realize that it is a part of God's nature. When the will of God is allowed to operate through our being, peace and ananda descend down. This is the wealth of Guru or God. Baba preaches sublimation and widening the base of mind and life energy to assimilate itself in God and His universe. As per Baba, broadening of mind means: purity, arousal of true love and knowledge, dhyana and nama recitation. Baba used to imply that God is to be remembered and worshipped in all walks of life. He cannot be limited to a shrine or mandir.

Baba's Approach to Sadhana

Baba used to view the entire life of a devotee as sadhana and not one single act of visiting a temple or doing an act of worship at a fixed place. The transformation of a whole jiva and its existence was Baba's aim in case of each devotee who approached him. The devotees or followers did not appreciate this holistic or comprehensive outlook of Baba, for they were not so mature or seasoned in the process of spiritual sadhana. Baba was the peak of spiritualism but they were still very raw and materialistic. They had noticed Sai Baba's miraculous powers and wanted to harness them to their own benefit. They were not much worried about

Sai Baba and Sadhana

higher spiritualism, service to humanity or uplift of mankind that Baba aimed at. They looked at Baba as an aulia or Vali, a miracle-mongering sadhu. They were not much concerned about his great mission of reforming humanity.

Baba's Way of Grace, Mission of Upliftment

Baba's style of imparting spiritual assistance was not reciting of mantra, asana, pranayam (breathing exercise), not even austere penance or other frantic rites or rituals. He therefore did not find any ashram or collected disciples or conducted schools for young and old aspirants. The first thing that Baba wanted to do was to clean the person internally and remove his lust for sansaric attachments. He could teach the person with direct or indirect words of knowledge and make him experience events in life, which could purify his nature and remove the dross of mundane and mayic ignorance in his bosom. He could use the whole world with the living and insentient creatures, stones, trees and animals as his medium of instruction. He was not an orthodox teacher but a divine guide, reformer of internal recesses of heart and soul. We do not judge or understand Baba fully because of our limited concepts about the Guruhood and the medium of spiritual instructions.

Words of Baba: Sadhana Reflected in Baba's Talks

Baba was a great Master of supreme spiritual status. Nobody can be compared with him. No man can be called as his disciple because his followers who thronged around him could never reach the maturity, depth and height. Even Upasani Maharaj who was a recognized spiritual figure could not be his full-fledged disciple. Baba told Upasani that even though he had given him a golden plate, it did not mean that he fully deserved to be Baba's replica. He also told Upasani that he had both punya purusha as well as paapa purusha in him. Baba was setting fire to the image of sin in Upasani. Baba had given high experiences to Upasani but he never allowed him to stay with him. He was kept away in Khandoba Temple and its precincts. However, it is a fact that Baba gave a bigger measure of grace to Upasani, who was kept away, than to Abdulla, Bhishma, Kushabhau, Nana, Ganu and Dabholkar. Baba, however, held Megha and Rege in higher esteem because he recognized the sentiment of the former and meditation of the latter. Really both of them were most fortunate to be so amply graced. These are different depths and heights of sadhana and readers are requested to note and understand this thoroughly for their benefit.

Story of Radhabai Deshmukh Desiring for Mantra from Sai Baba

Sai Baba's life story records Baba's reaction to an old lady trying to receive mantra from him as a Guru. Baba emphatically apprised her that his Guru had not taught him the cult to pass on Guru mantra to his disciples. His Guru never gave him any mantra. He received the dakshina in the form of faith, allegiance and dedication coupled with perseverance and tenacity to wait for grace. His Guru did not want puja, worship and karmic austerities. He wanted purity of mind and attitude of total surrender, which was the essence of bhakti. He rewarded such a deserving disciple with instant grace. He took charge of total life and existence of his disciple. Guru was a magnet that magnetized his disciple. He was the touchstone, which turned iron into gold by mere touch. The cult was of an instant grace. Baba graced his illiterate but dedicated bhakta Megha. Baba acknowledged the Vishnu dhyana of Justice Rege. There were rare devotees who earned a big measure of grace by their intrinsic merit of dedication, surrender and sincere love and application. They were aspirants but with a difference.

The Meditation of Guru Form

The educated, elite and positional men could not earn such grace from Baba because of their lack of depth and dedication. Baba approved concentration and meditation of the form of Guru as enjoined by Guru Geeta of Nath cult, which is approved by all sects like Nath, Kabir, Sufi and Dattatreya. Baba preferred meditation of form to recitation of name. In earlier incarnation as

Kabir, he was the advocate of Siddha name (surata-shabda). It was a great surprise that a great Master like Baba who was champion of instant grace did not get followers around him to receive his grace and the wealth of his Guru, which lay in abundance to shower upon the deserving and desirous. The sincerity and lack of receptivity marred the individuals around Baba to receive divine grace of earning moksha.

Merger in Cosmic Awareness through Grace

There is a vast difference between Baba's guidance and comments of philosophical commentators, who write wordy or verbal interpretations in philosophical texts. Baba works out his alchemy in a pure-minded, pious and sincere devotee whose mind, buddhi and ego are surrendered to God by raising his awareness from mundane level to higher level of piety, and discriminatory intellect to higher divine consciousness of cosmic mind. The cosmic and the individual awareness assimilate and operate uniformly and homogeneously. The mind which is delimited by the ego that speaks of 'I' and 'mine' imprints the selfish and tinted impressions of weal and woe, light and shade, victory and defeat and is tied down to lower interests of mundane life. The impressions of lust and attachment for power, money, luxury and fame are rubbed out by the touch of Baba's mercy. Thus Baba introduces us to divine life or sadhaka life. Baba wants us to merge into Satyam, Shivam and Sundaram. This is indeed the divine destination of the mankind which has lost its path in ignorance and wrong concepts. Baba's aim is to arouse divinity, auspiciousness, truth and symmetry in all walks of our life and all recesses of our existence. Baba's grace itself is the divine fragrance that covers all internal and external existence on this planet earth. Baba told Justice Rege to merge the mind and buddhi in each other and concentrate on Guru form sitting on the throne of heart. It is on the line of Guru Geeta saying—'Dhyanamoolam Gurormurti'. This includes all the nine forms of bhakti and transforms it into the atma nivedan bhakti, which is the essence of bhakti on the final summit of devotion process. The secret is blending atma nivedan bhakti with dhyana yoga of egoless surrender with stilled mind waves.

Baba and His Devotee World—The Cult of Nine-Fold Bhakti and Perpetual Meditation on Guru Form

This was what Baba preached. This shows how Baba looked at persons approaching him. To mundane bhaktas, he awarded gifts according to their merits and told them to act piously, follow truth and live a life of virtue to deserve the higher grace. To those who were partially purified, he enjoined them to faith and dedication to mould and transform their life to a more elevated stage. Those who purified their acts, thoughts, desire and ego, concentrated on Guru and God; those who served mankind without expectation of fruit, had unbiased leaning towards Guru and God. Baba favoured them with instant grace and lifted their consciousness to divine awareness. He treated each according to his level but never abandoned any who loved and cherished him, who sang his glory and acted as per his dictates or instructions. Kushabhau, Bhishma and Upasani were rare. Rege, Ganu, Chandorkar were elevated householder or spreaders of his mahima but were few and far in between. Most devotees and followers were of much lower level but Baba left none untouched. Even Abdulla, Mhalsapathi, Kote family members and Megha were loved by him on the score of their singular devotional attachment and faith towards him, not withstanding their ignorance or lack of educational stature. Baba read and saw through the hearts of his followers. He never looked at wealth, position, education, social stature of one who was drawn to him by love and faith. We are not able to view Baba properly in his genuine avataric and Guru stature. The words were not the only media he used to educate the people—vision, suggestion, indirect messages sent through other individuals, giving experiences of educative events were the many ways of teaching used by this Master and Guru incarnation.

Conflicting Ideas about Spiritualism

Against Sai Baba's sadhana teaching embracing core of spiritual truths, the attitude of a common man towards godheads and devotion is mechanical and as such it misses the true knowledge of spiritual process. It is therefore necessary for us to learn the truth from great Master like Baba, casting away our imitational concepts, which are apt to mislead us. Although great saints have spoken the truth, we fail to know and imbibe it in our mind. We still think that God dwells in mandirs and rituals and accept the middleman priest as God's agent. This is ignorance, we have to know, and worship God only by our own efforts and not through agents. Although idols give an idea of the godhead by partial presentation in stone, it is universally true that divinity does not stay in stone figures. Yet we spend so much money, effort and material in idol worship and erecting shrines. We must understand that idols are only symbolic. They have the divinity as long as we put our soul in them. The real temple of God is the body and the shrine is human heart (or awareness). Unless this inner God (cosmic awareness) is recognized and our consciousness is raised to its level and merged in, it cannot get realization. The process of raising human consciousness to divine consciousness is the real puja, yoga, dhyana or bhakti. Without this sadhana we cannot reach the destination of liberation or soul. Instead of doing puja in a secluded and protected place, we must turn our body, actions, speech, thoughts, emotions into godward sadhana. This is true liberation or moksha.

Reconciliation of Orthodox Ideas with Sai Thought

God is embedded in the human body and human consciousness. We have to carve out God from unconditioned form with the chisel of our sadhana seeking the ultimate truth. *Deha* (body) is temple and atma is God. But as our sight is turned outside, we do not see the Guru padukas or God's visitance above the eyebrow at trikuta point and siddha circle and beyond, leading us to Brahmanadi door. There lies the cave of sound or the flame of divine light at the place of the Bhramara Gumphal and Alaksha Niranjan Jyoti. We have forgotten that we have come to this earth as an onslaught of our karmas in past. To join the real or sterling experience of the self we have to see the God who is so proximate. 'The God is near and in the bosom but we do not meet him during entire life' is the saintly guidance. We have to join our mind to the cosmic one. Kabir revealed that his God lives in the breath and not in vales and dales. Baba says the same in different words. When lord Krishna said that he is present in the hearts of yogis and in the samkirtan of bhaktas, he pointed out that the heart consciousness of bhaktas installs him there, pulling him down from his Vaikuntha abode. When yogis meditate, Lord is present in their higher yogic consciousness, which lies above the mind, buddhi and pradnya points in the brain. Like Baba, Kabir and other realized saints renounced the stone idols and asked their devotees to locate God in the inner heart and brain circles united with God consciousness. He pointed out that the highest seat of God is above the weal and woe, sorrow and pleasure of mundane world. He said that his Sai dwelt inside prana or the movement of his vital airs. Kabir pointed out that the ignorance arising out of sense pleasures and selfish interests are to be removed to see the God who sits on the throne of heart hidden by these clouds of attachment and adhyana. Baba added to Kabir sadhana of recitation of divine name, the meditation of Guru form with absolute surrender and dedication of body mind, buddhi and ego. The love and the grace of Guru are the automatic gears, which left the soul to higher divine stature, where it can easily merge with divine consciousness of cosmic soul. We have dealt with this at length elsewhere in dealing with the life and philosophy of Sai Baba. Hence more detailed process of descent of kripa and merger with cosmic self is not attempted here.

Merger with God

If we have to find the truth of the existence, we have to cast all prejudices and also predilection and walk alone on the bridge of life and death undeterred by religious texts, old concepts, faiths, orthodox seals and religious limitations. The open mind and ego will reveal the truth. The truth is the same as love. Love is the same as light and the truth. Love, knowledge and God are all synonyms. The ultimate truth which saints, seers and Masters like Sai Baba have discovered is undeterred by faith, religion, sect, caste, creed and religious barriers.

How Sai Baba Guided Each According to His Atmic Level

We have discussed in general how Baba advised Upasani and Justice Rege as against less matured and uneducated men of faith like Megha and Abdul. We will go deeper now on how Baba loved all equally but had to teach them according to their preparation. To most Hindu and Muslim followers who surrounded him, Baba granted boons. He blessed them and cured many from their ailment and ill health. To some very near devotees, he used to distribute the dakshina money for their survival. Baba fed even animals and birds that flocked around the masjid. Baba knew that human beings cannot live on bread alone, hence he looked deeper into the future of his rustic followers and devotees living around in the hamlet Shirdi. His first followers were Mhalsapathi, Kashiram, Bala and Kote Patil family members. Their demands were only limited. They were not spiritual seekers. Baba increased their inner faith in God so that they realized that there is a divinity over and above the sansaric needs and day-to-day work. He told Kote Patil and devoted mother Baijabai that he was their father. They could ask for anything that they needed from him. They treated Baba as their son and fed him with bread and alms. This love for Baba helped them in developing their faith and treating Baba as God. He ultimately gave darshan of Lord Vishnu to them on their last journey. He saw that they evolve and get higher sadhaka status in their next birth, which would enable them to do higher sadhana for emancipation of their soul. This was the highest spiritual stage which they deserved. Balaram and Kashiram had faith in Baba as God, hence they held everything they received from Baba as God's own grace. Baba kept alive their faith by helping them in their occupation and personal life. Faith of Mhalsapathi was on still higher plane. He was the Khandoba priest and an austere devotee. Baba increased his faith by keeping him away from a luxuriant life. He never paid a single dakshina pie to Mhalsapathi even though the latter lived in utter poverty. By Baba's grace he accepted a deeper renounced life of an austere devotee who could sacrifice his mind, body, intellect and possession in the service of Khandoba. He held Baba as Shiva. Mhalsapathi was not educated or learned in religious lore but he was a fully dedicated soul living a poor, mundane life to deserve divine grace. Dengle, Gunda, Purandare and the contemporaries of Baba's earlier days were householders, respected men in society. Baba helped them to carry on their prapanch with piety, truth and honesty, so that they could progress on a graded devotional path and get gradual liberation. The trio, Mhalsapathi, Megha and Abdulla, who were of different nature, could represent the new category of old bhaktas, loyal to Baba yet had different spiritual depths and aptitudes. Out of the three, Megha was the chosen man whose orthodox ritualistic devotion was transformed by Baba to deep, intense bhakti of ideal stature.

Megha, Abdul and Mhalsapathi

The direction of Baba to these three are exemplary. Mhalaspathi was a priest, a householder and a poor man with faith and determination. Baba preached this priest that all godheads in the village should be equally respected and worshipped before he came to Baba for *his* puja. Baba did not overlook the hereditary priesthood of Mhalsapathi but directed him to discover the unity among godheads, not expecting money, wealth or returns for the worship. Baba taught him austerity, accepting whatever the destiny had given him and to do the duty with determination. This was ideal guidance to a karmic devotee who did not know higher tenets of atmic philosophy but was content in routine, rigid acts like puja, fasts and austerities. He would be joined to higher lokas, higher births and higher atmic ways of upasanas in the lives in store to achieve final emancipation. Abdul and Megha were rigid men of their religious orthodox faith. Baba taught them the unity of God, deep loyalty to Guru and the karmic upasanas they were following, so that their lives could be carried beyond the mayic sansar to the final destination by dint of their faith and loyalty to their Master. Both of them lived a life of seva and austerity. They treated Baba as Allah or Shiva and finally merged in him through Baba's grace. Baba had declared that these two had crossed the border.

Chandorkar, Ganu, Sathe, Dixit, Dabholkar

These devotees were men of education and stature in life. Ganu was a poet and kirtankar. They had essential background of knowledge of puranas, shastras and religious texts. They desired to be devoted and dedicated aspirants although they led a life in public affairs. Baba directed their learning and faith to advance in the proper devotional channel and to surrender all thoughts and actions to Guru so that the Master can lift them up through dhyana, bhakti and karma to the equivision of Geeta and Lord Krishna. Baba was their charioteer in sansara.

Bhishma, Kushabhau, Galwankar, Justice Rege, Upasani

They were advanced men of sadhana cult and Baba appreciated their essence of dhyana, which gave them higher experiences. The Guru cult of Sai Baba's Satchitananda Satguru form emanated in Shirdi, Maharashtra and thereafter on world plane through the stream of knowledgeable sadhakas of the last two categories.

The Inner Mystery of Sai Sadhana Teachings

The life of Sai Baba was clearly an example of a perfect soul. His life was a demonstration of Satyam, Shivam and Sundaram blended into one in human existence on this planet earth. It is therefore that his sadhana teachings are to be carved out of his words, deeds and life. The act, word and expression on Baba's face was only a fraction as compared with inner latent meaning, purpose and purport of Baba's brief words and exemplary deeds. Baba desired that his followers and devotees should transform their life into a pious one. Let us go deep into Baba's concept of Guruhood and Guru grace.

Uplifting Human Awareness to Divine Level

Baba knew all past, present and future of those who approached him. He knew their purity level, inner piety and future potential to rise above nature. Hence he could adjudge what advice would suit them, what reforms could change their level and lift them upwards to higher divine consciousness. Baba knew how they could be launched on the path of gradual emancipation through reformatory stages. He aimed at purifying both physical and psychological being of a devotee to make him fit to receive higher grace. Baba tried to diminish the distance between jiva and Shiva. He has made some to serve *jagat* (society) for the refinement of his jiva. His aim was to bring the purified consciousness near the higher divine awareness. Where there was no purification of body, mind, intellect and ego, Baba tried to reform them from the base level. He had to teach each according to his stage of evolution.

Cosmic Guru, Cosmic Awareness, Cosmic Mind

We can well interpret that Guru principle is synonymous with cosmic God or the universal divinity that creates, sustains and annihilates. The humanity is a part of this cosmic awareness but because of ignorance it has percolated or degenerated to mundane existence bound by the dimensions of time, space, ego as well as fettered by law of karma. Baba was identical with this principle in his higher divine state of Guruhood. His life, existence, words, speech and way of worship was in unison with the highest divine consciousness, which he in ordinary parlance would term as 'my Sarkar'. This Sarkar was his Dattatreya, Ram, Rahim or Allah. He was at once coexisting with him, as he existed in the entire sentient or non-sentient world of mountains, seas, forests, birds, animals, men and women. Baba's life was the representation of Guruhood as well as discipleship; it was at once descent of cosmic mind into human physical body. Many times he called himself as God. All other times he said that he was banda of Allah or a yadgar of Allah. This means that although the cosmic divinity was present in him and operating through him, he wanted to show that he was a different entity who came down to spread love, truth, knowledge and godliness.

The Astounding Manifestation of Guru

In Baba's earlier births like Shuka, Namdeo and Kabir he was a carrier of the cosmic message of truth, love and knowledge. One who knows Baba as the cosmic Satchitananda Guru knew him best. That was his real self or identity. Others mistook him as a fakir, vali, Siddha or sadhu for their limited purpose to derive mundane benefits from his siddha powers.

The Glory of Guru Sung by Baba

Baba has been incessantly singing the glory of Guru, although his birth was to postulate the stabilization, dissemination of the mahima of Guru. The constant concentration on Guru form, constant contemplation of the glory of Guru, incessant meditation on the awareness of Guru flows down the divine grace to earth. Baba selected Shirdi as his abode because his Sufi Guru had come to pass his last days in Shirdi under the neem tree. Baba's perpetual association with the memory of his Guru was his dedication and surrender. This was the essence of his Guru bhakti. This love is different from reading shastras, pothis, worship of idol, mantra–tantra, sacrifice, dhyana or pilgrimage.

Parallelism to World Thought of Great Thinkers

The cult of internal improvement and sublimation of individual soul to prepare it for the light of realization adopted by Baba has its parallelism with the thought of all great seers in the world. All the great souls had panted for the arrival of Krishna principle on earth. This yearning was met by Baba by his coming down to the mundane dust of earth to spread the philosophy of karma, dhyana, bhakti and yoga in the soil of the earth. It was understood by many that the divinity has finally descended on earth to meet the demands of the higher souls yearning to see the incarnation.

'One Who Knows My Divine Birth and Actions Is Freed'

It is correct what Geeta has said about the divine acts of lord. The incarnation or birth of divine on earth, its purpose, mission and philosophy has elevating force. This is because a person who knows or reveals this occult mystery is emancipated from the cycle of birth and death. To know Sai Baba's divine incarnation and its mission is itself a pathway to liberation. The lord of Geeta had made it already fully clear that people do not recognize the transcended God (incarnation) and are caught up in the maze of sansara and in the net of doubts. They forget the purpose of their being born on earth. When Guru incarnation comes down to earth, the mere meditation of his form, obedience to his orders and contemplation of his teachings itself becomes sadhana. It is in this strain that Baba told his evolved devotee Justice Rege to plant him in the heart and concentrate on him with mind and buddhi put together and surrender to him. The lord also has said in Geeta that devotees should concentrate on him, contemplate him and surrender their mind, intellect and ego to him. Then he would take them all beyond the ocean of sansara. This was indeed Baba's process of sadhana.

Guru, the Highest Status

Baba used to say that there was nobody who could fully know the mysterious power and supreme glory of his Guru (who was his Sarkar or Dattatreya). The sadhana of a devotee was only an effort to know this Satchitananda Guru form. The atma and paramatma cannot be known by itself. Atma can be translated into supreme self. These words itself and supreme self stand for individual and universal consciousness. The consciousness can know itself without organ, mind or thought. The transformation is automatic. The catalytic agent is self-sadhana plus grace. This truth is of universal spiritual value, which readers must learn fully. Atma cannot be known by outer methods, but the atma has the power to know itself. Vedanta therefore calls the atma as *swasamvedhya* (self-knowing). The atma, once it knows itself, can know the universal consciousness through the grace of Guru. The unity of individual consciousness with cosmic awareness is the final spiritual goal. The process is coming down of universal mind and rising up of individual consciousness. This is the aim of spiritual sadhana, whatever kind it may be. This process is inevitable in occultism. Coming down of divine consciousness is many times termed by saints, sages and masters as transcendence of grace. If the Guru element melts down to grace human consciousness, the process which is called sadhana, is made simple, beneficial and fruitful.

The Idea of Incarnation

It is said that God incarnates for the protection of good, and for the destruction of evil and establishment of the dharma. This means that when the world is full of impiety, loss of virtues and morality evil abides and the character declines, the Krishna element of cosmic Guruhood has to come down to save, uplift and transform humanity into divinity. If this is not done, the satanic elements will rule the earth forever. Sadhus and saints yearn for the advent of the supreme and the cosmic responds to the prayer of sages and munis. Saints and Masters like Sai are such incarnations of the supreme that come down to save and elevate the erring and faltering human race. Baba aims at creation of faith in Guru and God, pious and good actions of selfless service to establish the base for the transcendence. He desires that a devotee's entire life should be pure, moral, sincere, full of faith and service so that God could plant His foot in that pious heart.

Teaching Style of Sai Baba

The sadhana thoughts expressed by Sai Baba are not like a treatise or a book written specially for readers. The thoughts, which have been recorded by us, are like flowers woven in a garland from the scattered, occasional and event-inspired expressions of Baba, collected and arranged in a particular format. We have to read them with understanding and benefit ourselves from the honey and the fragrances latent in the flowers. If we look at Baba as a fakir of miraculous deeds and astounding siddhis, we shall not be able to understand him. Real understanding of spiritual sadhana does not lie in the learned lectures and sermons of erudite scholars. The sadhana is to be gathered from the company, lifestyle and the sporadic expressions made by Sai Baba's order and stature. Baba did not give importance to mantras, japas, fasts and austerities. He wanted one's whole life and psychological stature to be purified and elevated. Baba's spiritual concept was not based on the worship of idols, visiting temples and mosques. He wanted us to transform our body into a shrine for Guru or God to descend and sojourn. The God to be sought in the vital breath of the heart and to be installed in the consciousness in such a way that individual awareness no longer remains to be materialistic and mundane consciousness but lifted up while merging in cosmic consciousness. Where the mind and breath unites, the light of atma flourishes. We have to light the inner flame with the spark of the grace that emanates from the compassion of Guru. The Guru always blesses a dedicated and surrendered soul. The aim of all sadhanas is to turn life into perfection. This will transform not only an individual but the entire society, the entire world.

■ ■ ■

Our books on Shirdi Sai Baba

Shirdi Sai Baba is a household name in India as well as in many parts of the world today. These books offer fascinating glimpses into the life and miracles of Shirdi Sai Baba and other Perfect Masters. These books will provide you with an experience that is bound to transform one's sense of perspective and bring about perceptible and meaningful spiritual growth.

SHRI SAI SATCHARITA
The Life and Teachings of Shirdi Sai Baba
Translated by Indira Kher
ISBN 81 207 2211 6   Rs. 500 (HB)
ISBN 81 207 2153 5   Rs. 300 (PB)

BABA- May I Answer
C.B. Satpathy
ISBN 978 81 207 45940
Rs. 150

Sri Narasimha Swami
Apostle of Shirdi Sai Baba
Dr. G.R. Vijayakumar
ISBN 978 81 207 4432 5
Rs. 90

Spotlight on the Sai Story
Chakor Ajgaonker
ISBN 81 207 4399 1   Rs. 200

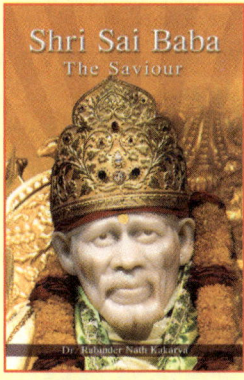

Shri Sai Baba-The Saviour
Dr. Rabinder Nath Kakarya
ISBN-978-81-207-4701-2
Rs. 75

Shri Sai Baba-The Divine Healer
Raj Chopra
ISBN-978-81-207-4632-9
Rs.100

Shirdi Sai Baba and
Other Perfect Masters
C B Satpathy
ISBN 978 81 207 2384 8 Rs. 135

I am always with you
Lorraine Walshe-Ryan
ISBN 81 207 3192 9 Rs. 150

Unravelling the Enigma
Marrianne Warren
ISBN 81 207 2147 0 Rs. 400

God Who Walked on Earth:
The Life & Times
of Shirdi Sai Baba
R Parthasarathy
ISBN 81 207 1809 7 Rs. 95

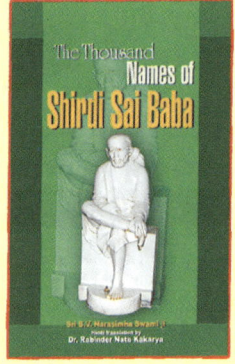
The Thousand Names of
Shirdi Sai Baba
Sri B.V. Narasimha Swami Ji
ISBN 978 81 207 3738 9 Rs. 75

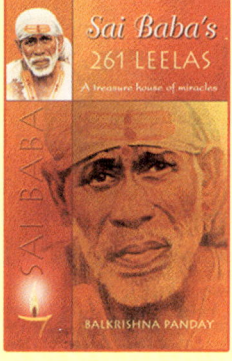
Sai Baba's 261 Leelas
Balkrishna Panday
ISBN 81 207 2727 4 Rs. 75

108 Names of Shirdi Sai Baba
ISBN 81 207 3074 8
Rs. 50

Sri Swami Samarth –
Maharaj of Akkalkot
N. S. Karandikar
ISBN 978 81 207 3445 6 Rs. 200

Guru Charitra
Shree Swami Samarth
ISBN 978 81 207 3348 0 Rs. 200

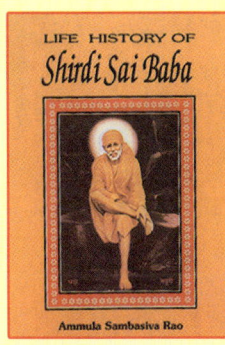

Life History of Shirdi Sai Baba
Ammula Sambasiva Rao
ISBN 81 207 2033 4
Rs. 95

A Solemn Pledge
from True Tales of Shirdi Sai Baba
Dr B H Briz-Kishore
ISBN 81 207 2240 x
Rs. 95 (Also available in Hindi, Tamil, Kannada & Telugu)

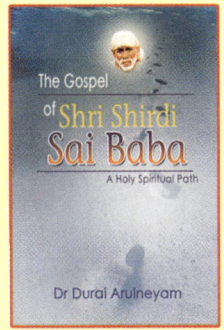

The Gospel of Shri Shirdi Sai Baba: A Holy Spiritual Path
Dr Durai Arulneyam
ISBN 978 81 207 3997 0
Rs. 150

Shri Shirdi Sai Baba: His Life and Miracles
ISBN 81 207 2877 7 Rs. 25

Shri Sai Baba's Teachings & Philosophy
Lt Col M B Nimbalkar
ISBN 81 207 2364 3 Rs. 75

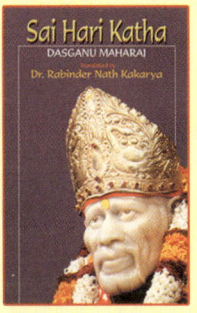

Sai Hari Katha
Dasganu Maharaj
ISBN 978 81 207 3324 4
Rs. 75

Sai Baba: His Divine Glimpses
V B Kher
ISBN 81 207 2291 4 Rs. 95

Sri Sai Baba
Sai Sharan Anand
ISBN 81 207 1950 6 Rs. 125

Shirdi Sai Speaks...
Sab Ka Malik Ek
Quotes for the Day
ISBN 81 207 3101 8 Rs. 200
(Also available in Hindi)

Baba's Rinanubandh:
Leelas during His Sojourn
in Shirdi
Compiled by Vinny Chitluri
ISBN 81 207 3403 6   Rs. 200

Baba's Vaani: His Sayings
and Teachings
Compiled by Vinny Chitluri
ISBN 978 81 207 3859 1 Rs. 200

Baba's Gurkul SHIRDI
Vinny Chitluri
ISBN-978-81-207-4770-8
Rs. 200

साई हरि कथा
दासगणु महाराज
ISBN 978 81 207 3323 7 Rs. 65

साई–सबका मालिक
कल्पना भाकुनी
ISBN 978 81 207 3320 6 Rs.100

साई दत्तावधूता
राजेन्द्र भण्डारी
ISBN 81 207 4404 1 Rs. 75

श्री शिरडी साई बाबा व अन्य सद्गुरू
चन्द्रभानु सतपथी
ISBN 81 207 4401 1 Rs. 90

बाबा आध्यात्मिक विचार
चन्द्रभानु सतपथी
ISBN 978-81-207-4627-5
Rs. 150

बाबा की वाणी उनके वचन तथा उपदेश
बेला शर्मा
ISBN 978-81-207-4745-6
Rs. 100

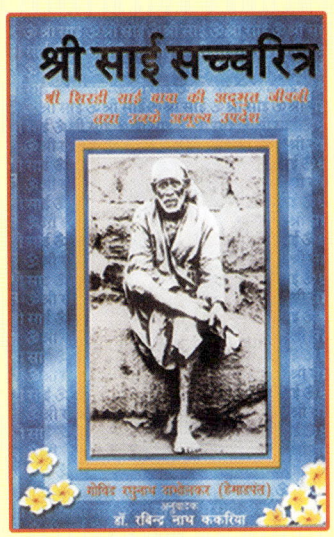

श्री साईं सच्चरित्रा
डॉ रबिन्द्र नाथ ककरिया
ISBN 81 207 2501 8 Rs. 250 (PB)
ISBN 81 207 2500 X Rs. 300 (HB)

साईं शरण में
चन्द्रभानु सतपथी
ISBN 81 207 2802 5 Rs. 100

पृथ्वी पर अवतरित भगवान
शिरड़ी के साईं बाबा
रंगास्वामी पार्थसारथी
ISBN 81 207 2101 2 Rs. 95

श्री साईं बाबा के परम भक्त
डॉ रबिन्द्र नाथ ककरिया
ISBN 81 207 2779 7 Rs. 75

श्री नरसिम्हा स्वामी
शिरडी साईं बाबा के दिव्य प्रचारक
डॉ रबिन्द्र नाथ ककरिया
ISBN 978 81 207 4437 0   Rs. 75

शिरडी साईं बाबा
प्रो डॉ बी एच ब्रिज़–किशोर
ISBN 81 207 2346 5   Rs. 60

साईं का संदेश
डॉ रबिन्द्र नाथ ककरिया
ISBN 81 207 2879 3   Rs. 90

मुक्तिदाता श्री साईं बाबा
डॉ रबिन्द्र नाथ ककरिया
ISBN 81 207 2778 9   Rs. 60

साई भक्तानुभव
डॉ. रबिन्द्र नाथ ककरिया
ISBN 978 81 207 3052 6 Rs. 90

श्री साई बाबा के अनन्य भक्त
डॉ रबिन्द्र नाथ ककरिया
ISBN 81 207 2705 3 Rs. 75

शिरडी संपूर्ण दर्शन
डॉ रबिन्द्र नाथ ककरिया
ISBN 81 207 2312 0 Rs. 50

शिरडी साई के दिव्य वचन
सबका मालिक एक
ISBN 978 81 207 3533 0 Rs. 180

Shirdi Sai Baba (Kannada)
Prof. Dr.B.H. Briz Kishore
ISBN 81 207 2873 4 Rs. 60

Shirdi Sai Baba (Telugu)
Prof. Dr.B.H. Briz Kishore
ISBN 81 207 2294 9 Rs. 60

Shirdi Sai Baba (Tamil)
Prof. Dr.B.H. Briz Kishore
ISBN 81 207 2876 9 Rs. 60

For detailed Catalogue visit our website
www.sterlingpublishers.com
E-mail:mail@sterlingpublishers.com